TRADITIONAL RHYMING POEMS & SHORT STORIES

Volume 1

TRADITIONAL RHYMING POEMS & SHORT STORIES

Volume 1

Wayne B. Bowman

The Waterfall Poet

Other than a few of the authors relatives, the names and characters in this book are fictional, and in no way intended to represent any person, living or dead.

© Copyright 2022 Wayne B. Bowman

All rights reserved. No part of this book may be reproduced or transmitted in any form whatsoever without prior written permission of the author, except in the case of brief quotations embodied in pertinent articles and reviews.

Dedication:

I dedicate this book to my mom and dad, (Bernie and Esther) whom have gone on to be with the Lord. They are my heroes. I miss them every day.

FOREWORD

I'm just a small-town country boy with no college education. That fact goes a long way in explaining the vernacular in this book. I speak country.

It has taken almost two years for this book to come to fruition. Lots of delays along the way, but that's just part of life no matter what you do for a living, or for a hobby. It took me nine years to finish my first book, so I won't complain.

The following is a collection of around eighty or so poems, song lyrics and short stories I'd like to share with my readers. It is my wish they will perhaps lift your spirits, lighten your load or at the very least bring a smile to your face, or a chuckle to your heart.

CHAPTER 1

THE FUNNY BONE

1 FLYIN' BY THE SEAT OF MY PANTS!

3 MY GRANNY

4 GRANDPAS' STILL

6 HALLOWEEN NIGHT

7 WHAT YEAR IS THIS?

9 THE WILL

11 AUNT MOLLIE'S TROLLEY

13 DO YOU KNOW WHO I AM?

15 JUST A SILLY CHIPMUNK

17 THINGS THAT MAKE ME SMILE -1

19 THINGS THAT MAKE ME SMILE -2

21 THE BULLY

22 THE FALL

23 OUCH

24 OLD BEFORE MY TIME

25 HAS ANYBODY SEEN MY HAIR?

26 SOME BIRTHDAY THOUGHTS

28 RANDOM THOUGHTS

31 STUPID STUFF

32 MUDDY WATER

34 WHO KNEW DIDDLY-DOO?

36 TAKE MY ADVICE

37 THE FAN-ATTIC

39 BUGS

40 NAP TIME

CHAPTER 2
ANYTHING GOES

42 A TIME OF REFLECTION

43 OLD DOC'

44 I REMEMBER WHEN

45 IT'S ABOUT TIME

48 MY HOME IN TENNESSEE

50 STORMY DAY DREAMS

52 FACE IN THE MIRROR

54 THE WALL

55 THE POET

56 THE HUMMINGBIRD

59 HE'S A CRAFTSMAN

60 THE EXPEDITION

61 THE GOOD ONES ARE GONE

62 WHO AM I?

63 THE TROUBLE WITH KIDS TODAY

64 THE OLD FIVE AND DIME

66 A VOICE IN THE NIGHT

67 ENOUGH IS ENOUGH

69 THE OLD MAN FROM THE MOUNTAIN

71 TRUCK DRIVER SURVIVOR

73 MISTER ENGINEER

CHAPTER 3

FROM THE HEART

76 THE LAST THING I SEE
78 NOT WHAT YOU EXPECTED
79 ONE MORE DAY
80 DOES IT REALLY MATTER ANYMORE?

81 THINKING OF YOU

82 THE OLD GUITAR
84 MEMORIES

86 BLINK OF AN EYE

87 THE LISTENER

99 THE OLD WOODSHOP

CHAPTER 4

FROM THE SOUL

93 THE WHISPER
94 ROSES AND THORNS
96 THE OTHER SIDE OF LIFE
97 I AM BLESSED
98 WHEN WILL I LEARN?
99 WHEN MY TIME HAS COME
100 WHEN THINGS COME UNDONE

101 WALK ON THE WATER
102 HE WILL LEAD THE WAY
104 THE ANSWER
105 THE TRUE MEANING OF CHRISTMAS
107 MORNING PRAYERS
109 WHAT WOULD YOU DO IF---
111 A BETTER PLACE
112 MY BEST ADVICE

CHAPTER 5

POETIC SHORT STORIES

114 THE FRONT PORCH SWING

121 THE LAST SUNSET

125 AN OLD RUSTY FORD

129 THE MAN FROM TENNESSEE

131 THE BEGINNING AND THE END

135 THE OLD JUNK MAN

CHAPTER 6

SONG LYRICS

139 TENNESSEE BACKROADS

142 PROXIMO

144 A WING AND A PRAYER
146 HIS NAME WAS JESUS
148 WHAT HAPPENED TO MY COUNTRY?
151 HIS NEVER-ENDING LOVE

152 A COUNTRY CHRISTMAS
154 THERE IS A MOUNTAIN
155 ENGINEER BLUES

CHAPTER 7

FICTIONAL SHORT STORIES

158 THE GHOST OF MAGGIE VALLEY

TRADITIONAL RHYMING POEMS & SHORT STORIES

CHAPTER 1

THE FUNNY BONE

FLYIN' BY THE SEAT OF MY PANTS!

When I was young, Mrs. Poteet lived across the street.

She was sweet as she could be.

But her bulldog named Chance, bit the seat out of my pants,

when he tried to take a bite out of me.

Well, as happened one day, a fly ball got away,

and landed smack dab in her tree.

Heads or tails, and odd man out,

determined the fetcher was me.

So, I ventured in to retrieve that stray,

not knowing I'd regret that very day.

Half way across her yard I realized,

I was being watched by those piercing eyes.

Then, the sound of charging feet.

To the gate, a hasty retreat.

To the fence instead, taking to the air

proved a little too slow, for my derriere.

Landing in the street on both my feet,

to resounding laughter at my defeat.

Reaching for my back pant pocket, how dense,

WAYNE B. BOWMAN

for I'd left it, on the other side of the fence.

Now that ball again, we never did see.

And to this day, I remember with a sigh,

for what happened in that yard, I tell you now,

gave new meaning to the term- -sacrifice fly.

TRADITIONAL RHYMING POEMS & SHORT STORIES

MY GRANNY

Now, my Granny was something else.

Let me tell you why.

She drove a forty-nine Ford and man, she could fly.

Now, that ride was clean and a runnin' machine.

Fire engine red, with bright yellow stripes,

fender skirts and chrome lake pipes.

Now, she could shoot straighter than most men could,

and tell you all about what was under that hood.

She had a jug tucked away in the back of that car,

said it saved her from havin' to stop at a bar.

Under the seat was stashed an old 45.

Told me one night in Texas, it kept her alive.

I heard her cuss, and saw her smoke cigars,

and drink moonshine from Mason jars.

Settin' at the table with a dead man's hand,

and a poker face that would fool any man.

She travelled this land from coast to coast.

Had more cool stories than most could boast.

Found a way to make a livin' wherever she'd go,

From Maine all the way to Mexico.

Now, Granny's been gone for quite some time,

and I'm grateful for all these memories.

So, now you know why I wrote this rhyme.

GRANDPA'S STILL

My Grandpa had a big ole' still,

behind a big ole' rock up on the hill.

He would run it throughout the night.

It was pretty much a pitiful sight.

Now, there were pipes running here,

Copper coils running there.

Big barrels all set in a row.

It would huff and puff, toot and whistle.

He would laugh and say,

I didn't build it for show ya' know!

"I'll trade a pint for a chicken anytime, son."

The eggs from that bird would recover the cost,

of making that run.

Deep in the forest, all tucked out of sight,

Grandpa filled jars until the first light.

Everywhere barrels of corn rendering.

If the revenuer drops in,

Gramp's will drop out.

TRADITIONAL RHYMING POEMS & SHORT STORIES

Cause, they ain't no way he's surrendering.

This illegal trade that he did partake

Knowing someday he'd make a mistake

Disappearing for days was just his way.

Grandma would just smile,

Don't worry she would say.

He'll be back in a little while.

Grandpa is gone now,

But I think of him often.

I know he's surely smilin',

cause I dropped a pint in his coffin.

WAYNE B. BOWMAN

HALLOWEEN NIGHT

Ghosts, goblins, and monsters galore

prowling the neighborhoods door to door.

Ballerinas, butterflies, and Kermit the frog,

On this dark gloomy night adrift with dense fog.

Ominous clouds rolling overhead.

Blood curdling screams

waking up the dead.

Candy corn and apples,

milk duds and goobers.

Frankenstein, and the Mummy

just stepped out of an Uber.

Witches on broom sticks,

black cats in a tree.

Some houses brightly lit.

Others, dark as can be.

Only one night each year, you see

that they all can go crazy

and be anything they want to be.

It's midnight now and the streets are clear.

But fear not my pretty's.

For they'll all be back

this same time next year.

TRADITIONAL RHYMING POEMS & SHORT STORIES

WHAT YEAR IS THIS?

Would somebody please explain to me,

exactly what a smart phone is supposed to be.

And, what on earth is google?

By chance the opposite of frugal?

Emoji, app's, Wi-Fi, and 5G?

All I can say is, "Beats the heck out of me."

I've heard of something called Email,

And also, something called a text.

A phone I can take pictures with.

What will they think of next?

911 is something new.

Same for those little lines they call a sku'.

Keeping in mind that I'm way behind

on all this technology,

Someday you know they'll be telling me,

this phone can send a photo to Tennessee.

A rocket scientist, I'm am not,

But they tell me this stuff is really hot.

Megabytes, gigabytes and terabytes too.

Every time I turn around, it's something new.

Too confusing for someone, so out of touch,

WAYNE B. BOWMAN

my brain is all foggy, this is way too much.

This thing called a cell phone amazes me so.

My old phone was connected to a wire you know.

Now I can take my phone with me where ever I go.

"Did you just crawl out of a cave?" she asked me.

No mam, I've been in a coma since 1963.

Keeping in mind that I'm way behind

On all this technology,

They say they hate spam, which I just fail to see.

I had some for dinner last night-----

or was that in 63.

TRADITIONAL RHYMING POEMS & SHORT STORIES

THE WILL

The "WILL," was plain and simple.

I believe it made it clear.

Of whom the departed was wary,

and those he held so dear.

A most generous man was Henri,

to a fault I truly say,

but, upon his demise,

his eight kids and eight wives,

protested with pretentious display.

To his servant Sally,

he left quite a tally,

enough to choke a horse they say.

Those who know her well,

say to one she did tell,

she'd lost half on Derby Day.

Now to his barber Hank,

I'm told he left quite a sum.

I'm not really sure,

but he left and went straight to the bank.

A sizable sum for his butler Poke,

who was always there when needed,

WAYNE B. BOWMAN

A true friend was he indeed,

and always so quick with a joke.

To his youngest he left his Bentley,

o the next he left his yacht.

For the other six, he really got his kicks,

by leaving them worthless stocks.

Now to his eight wives, he left nothing,

which left them all huffing and puffing.

Now what I still have to say,

will surely blow you away.

For to all their dismay,

everything else, went to the SPCA.

TRADITIONAL RHYMING POEMS & SHORT STORIES

AUNT MOLLY'S TROLLEY

My uncle Ollie, and dear aunt Molly,

lived in a converted old trolley.

Truly something to see.

It was quite a site,

when at last it took flight,

on a flatbed from Tennessee.

According to my mother,

when it came up for auction,

they bid without caution.

At times against one another.

The inside an eclectic mix,

of amazing artistic tricks.

Crystal chandeliers,

with tiny glass spheres,

hung from the ceiling at nine foot six.

Gas lanterns lighted the halls.

Filigree embossed the walls.

Cowhide upholstered seats,

On the bed lay blue satin sheets.

The exterior was black, red and white,

which was quite a contrasting site.

With the wheels painted an orange as bright,

as pumpkins on Halloween Night.

People said, surely, they must be batty,

when they arrived back in Cincinnati.

But before too long,

they'd be changing their song,

when out stepped uncle Ollie,

to hang up a sign that read,

"OLLIE & MOLLY'S HOT DOG TROLLY."

And the city hence forth enjoyed being fed.

DO YOU KNOW WHO I AM

What's my name?
Sure wish I knew.
So, what's yours?
Should I remember you?
They say I had a terrible fall.
Quite a spill you see.
Can't remember that at all,
but then, can't even remember me.
Guess I'll have to take their word,
it will all come back some day.
But for now, I sit and wonder,
why it even went away.
Can't tell you where I'm from,
or where I was going to.
What month this is,
or anything else that I once knew.
Don't know if I had a plan,
or even where I am.
Thought I heard someone say,
"Maybe he's running away."
Running away, did you say?

WAYNE B. BOWMAN

Like a criminal with a plan.

If there's any truth to that,

I hope I stay right where I am.

For evil, is not my wish to be.

A man on the run,

Never truly to be free.

But, can I live the rest of my life,

never knowing, if in my past

there are children, and a wife.

A mom and dad who may wonder,

if they'll ever again see their son.

Not knowing if he's even safe,

or an outlaw on the run.

Maybe one day I'll find a way,

to return to the life I use to know.

But, for now I'll have to be content

to be known to one and all, as, John Doe.

JUST A SILLY CHIPMUNK

I'm just a silly chipmunk;

I suppose you could say.

I scamper around the campgrounds all day.

Darting here and popping up there.

Appearing not to have a single care.

Up a tree, then down the fence,

making little, if any sense.

Peeking from under some leaves to see

who in the world is laughing at me.

Chasing the birds away from the seed,

hoarding it ever so selfishly.

Stuffing nuts in both cheek's til' I almost explode.

Then I hurry back for another load.

If you could follow to see, where it is that I go,

it's my underground storehouse, I hope you know.

Filled from end to end, and left to right.

My, oh my, what a beautiful site.

Though they think up there I play every day,

and that I'm silly for storing so much away.

But there is something that they don't realize.

Their cat wants to eat me, I see it in his eyes.

So, I've created a place where I can hide

when no longer it is safe upon the topside.

far away from his glaring eyes,

where I can stay until the day he dies.

Oh my! What is this I see?

Has his time on earth finally come to an end?

For a better view I must climb a tree.

Oh no! what have they done to me?

They buried that stupid cat on top of my den.

Now I must start all over again.

My friend the chipmunk. Saying his prayers.

TRADITIONAL RHYMING POEMS & SHORT STORIES

THINGS THAT MAKE ME SMILE -1

I like things that make me smile.

If only for a little while.

Things that catch me by surprise,

then gone before I realize.

Children playing with Silly String.

How cute, such a simple thing.

The senior couple walking on the sand,

enjoying the sunset, hand in hand.

The loving stare of two newlyweds,

some things they know need not be said.

The old man down the street,

who for some reason thinks my name is Pete.

Butterflies fluttering from flower to flower.

Children watching them hour after hour.

Two squirrels chasing a cat,

one so skinny, the other so fat.

A woodpecker pecking on a metal flag pole,

not even a dent, much less a hole.

The bus driver singing Wheels on the Bus Go Round,

as he chauffer's people all over town.

The car salesman who says, "That's our absolute lowest price."

WAYNE B. BOWMAN

If only his nose would grow, wouldn't that be nice.

Lyrics to a funny song,

that make me chuckle, as I hum along.

An officer stopping to lend a hand,

changing a tire for an elderly man.

Some teens helping a turtle across the road.

Concern for the helpless, to their credit you know.

It feels so good to smile,

so, carry one with you wherever you go.

Share it here, share it there,

show others you really care.

So, when you see an opportunity,

and they'll come along now and then, you see.

Take advantage, make it worth your while.

Take the time to make someone smile.

TRADITIONAL RHYMING POEMS & SHORT STORIES

THINGS THAT MAKE ME SMILE -2

I like things that make me smile,

if only for a little while.

Two puppies playing tug-of-war,

dragging one another across the floor.

A grown man playing on a Slip-N-Slide.

First on his belly, then his backside.

A little boy eating an ice cream cone,

on a hot summer day, barely holding his own.

A baby with his foot in his mouth,

looking ever so puzzled while he figures it out.

Little children chasing fire flies.

Grandma watching with a gleam in her eyes.

The mailman running down the street,

My neighbors chihuahua nipping at his feet.

A friend of mine who's afraid of snakes.

First, she screams, and then she shakes.

A picnic beneath the old oak tree.

Nobody in sight, just you and me.

A sno-cone on a hot summer day.

Grandpa coming out to play.

A little girl holding baby brother's hand.

WAYNE B. BOWMAN

Crystal blue surf gently washing the sand.

Penney candy in a small-town store.

Girl Scouts selling cookies at my front door.

Now, thanks for listening, what more can I say,

Except, try to make someone smile today.

TRADITIONAL RHYMING POEMS & SHORT STORIES

THE BULLY

He can't help but wonder why they pick on him.

Always by himself, never messing with them.

Kind of small, not very tall.

Never looking for trouble at all.

He hates to fight, so will try to walk away.

Turning the other cheek, is all he will say.

A bloody nose, cut on his face,

to so many, would be a disgrace.

Detours, he would often take,

trying to avoid his likely fate.

One day though they'll make a mistake,

when perhaps he's had, all he can take.

His friends all know there'll come that day,

when he'll decide not to walk away.

In the mean time they wait patiently,

hoping they'll be there just to see,

when the bullies finally get their due.

That's when he'll teach them a lesson or two.

For what these bullies don't seem to know,

he's a third-degree black belt, in Tai Kwon Do.

WAYNE B. BOWMAN

THE FALL

A twenty-foot fall from a tree,

has made a mental mess out of me.

I landed on my head,

and by all rights should be dead,

but instead, it messed up my memory.

Sometimes off and sometimes on.

Organizational skills pretty much gone.

Confusing to say the least.

Virtue of patience mostly deceased.

You-- see things in order, like ABC's,

things mostly mixed up to me.

Can't help it, just the way I am.

If it doesn't make sense,

My brain just moves it to spam.

TRADITIONAL RHYMING POEMS & SHORT STORIES

OUCH!

Sometimes I like to grow a beard,

much to the wife's dismay.

She says that I'm strangely weird.

Is it possible I am that way?

She claims that I'm just lazy,

but that's not the case you see.

I'm just not really into things,

that make a bloody mess of me.

Double edge, straight edge and electrics I've tried.

Foams, powders and bracers too.

So difficult to decide,

So, tell me, what would you do?

She also complains it scratches,

whenever she kisses me.

Oh! Now she's really upset,

since I said, then just leave me be.

Long beard, short beard, makes no difference, you see.

For unless I'm totally beard free,

she won't be seen with me.

So, here's what I've been thinking about.

A solution I think, you'll see.

One by one I'll just pull them out,

painful as it may be.

OLD BEFORE MY TIME

Each day vanishes much faster than it used to.

Breakfast, lunch, dinner and off to bed.

Not enough time for things I want to do.

Visions of tomorrows adventures dance in my head.

Same routine as the day before,

Is this Thursday or Friday?

Who's keeping score?

Today I'll do things my way.

I think it's a cave I'll explore.

After all, if I'm down there,

What can they say?

Oh no! In trouble again, yes, I am.

All because of "Big Mouth Sam."

On my way to a labyrinth underground,

When stopped at the corner by officer Spence,

who promptly turned me around.

"Back you go," he said with a grin.

"And don't let me catch you out here again.

This is becoming a habit." So said he.

Next time I'm going to Tennessee.

HAS ANYBODY SEEN MY HAIR

When I was young, I had a full head of hair.

And today, there's scarcely any there.

Receding to the back, ever so slow.

Will it ever grow back, I really don't know?

So many years later now.

One look in the mirror, "OH, WOW!"

So little did I know,

just how fast it would go.

When I ask if she's seen my hair,

she laughs and says, it's everywhere.

It's on the floor, it's in the hall,

on the sofa and on the chair.

The sweeper is cloggin,'

with the hair from your noggin.

With a crackle and a spark,

it burned up the Shark.

So, now in despair,

over the loss of my hair.

No longer will I ask where it's at.

I think I'll just buy me a hat.

SOME BIRTHDAY THOUGHTS

The older I get; the less birthdays mean to me.

After all, it's just a number, so some people say.

What's all the fuss, I just fail to see.

So far, I feel no different than yesterday.

I used to hear, "Wait until you reach forty."

Forty came and went without notice.

Then I heard, "Wait until you reach fifty."

So, fifty is gone, and I haven't a clue.

Now, I'm seventy-two and I don't know what I'm to do.

I creak and groan, and pop and crack.

I forget what I was about to say,

as my mind is constantly losing track.

And sometimes, I lose my way.

My hairs no longer where it used to be.

Having misplaced my glasses,

makes it so hard to see.

I can't find my teeth.

My right shoes on my left foot,

and the left one is on my right.

My biceps are flabbin,'

and my belly is saggin.'

When I first get up, I'm a pitiful site.

So, now you can see,

why it's so hard for me

to admit they eventually got it right.

WAYNE B. BOWMAN

RANDOM THOUGHTS

From time to time,

random thoughts come to mind.

Sometimes out of the blue,

when I have nothing to do.

These thoughts sometimes so very strange.

No boundaries, limits or controlling range.

It's anything goes,

and heaven only knows,

as my brain goes hippity hop,

cause once it starts, it just won't stop.

Now, where are they taking me?

Is this a hotel?

Everyone is dressed in white.

Somethings surely not right.

What's wrong with my brain? Am I going insane?

Will this someday all come to an end?

I really don't know, and so,

until then, I'll just have to pretend.

I'll fake it, and so,

they'll never really know.

They'll never suspect a thing.

TRADITIONAL RHYMING POEMS & SHORT STORIES

Where is everybody?

Hello, hello! Could somebody please check me in?

Testing and prodding, and probing they've done.

I want to leave, but they've only begun.

An MRI of my brain,

will prove I'm not really insane.

Is there any hope I'll survive?

To once again mentally thrive?

Or will stress take its toll,

and destroy my soul,

and random thoughts be in control?

Behind closed doors,

they add up my scores.

Now, they say the jury's still out,

for quite a while, no doubt.

As they exit the room,

I can only assume,

they've reached a conclusion for sure.

Am I free to go home,

and live all alone,

or is this my home forever more?

Their shaking their heads.

That can't be good!

WAYNE B. BOWMAN

I really don't want to live in this neighborhood.

The doctors say what they find,

well-- they really aren't sure,

If I'm insane, or just out of my mind.

TRADITIONAL RHYMING POEMS & SHORT STORIES

STUPID STUFF

I'm just sittin' here, lookin' all about,

just tryin' to figure this crazy rhyme out.

Really don't know what I'm supposed to do,

if nothin' comes to mind.

Stressing out over lack of rhyme.

Relax man, just give it time.

Can't think of anything but stupid stuff.

Maybe that's the answer.

Maybe that's enough.

Crazy thoughts coursing through my brain,

making very little sense.

Perhaps I'm going insane!

I close my eyes and begin to dream,

of silly and ridiculous things, it seems.

Squirrels, birds, rabbits and pigs,

wearing crazy clothes and goofy wigs.

A chicken all dressed in red.

A monkey in pink leotards.

A cow with a hat on her head,

drinking beer and smoking cigars.

Should I write about something nice?

WAYNE B. BOWMAN

Do you think that would be good enough?

Or take my crazy friend's advice,

and just write about stupid stuff?

MUDDY WATER

"What on Earth were you thinking?"

She said to me one day,

standing there in the pouring rain,

as her red Mini Cooper drifted away.

The water appeared only a few inches deep.

Wouldn't have been bad if in my Jeep.

Buoyancy, the dominating rule,

making me look like such a fool.

The rain came down for days on end.

We thought we'd never see sun again.

Day after day we prayed for a drought.

Seemed the only solution to drying things out.

When the rain finally came to a stop,

Everything was coated in slop.

Never seen anything like this before.

I couldn't even open the door.

There's a lesson here to be learned.

TRADITIONAL RHYMING POEMS & SHORT STORIES

Things aren't always as they seem.

Think twice before jumping in,

to that swift and muddy stream.

Safety comes first and always,

as I'm sure that you may know.

Don't be like the Mini Cooper,

and get swept up in the flow.

The good news is she forgave me,

And claims she'll soon forget,

Just as soon as she's driving her new car,

A shiny red Corvette.

WAYNE B. BOWMAN

WHO KNEW DIDDLY-DOO?

Who knew Diddly-Doo?

His dog Skippy, and his sister, Boo.

You never know what Diddly will do.

Hard to figure out just what he's up to.

Riding his scooter all over town,

or selling lemonade dressed up like a clown.

Swinging on a rope dangling from a tree,

screaming at the top of his lungs, "I'm free, I'm free!"

Floating down the river in a canoe built for two,

capsized in the rapids, poor Diddly-Doo.

Being chased down the street by a neighbor's hound dog,

then back up the street by a pot-bellied hog.

Usually in trouble for somethin' he's done.

Seems like Diddly's always on the run.

He has a big heart, this little lad,

always laughing, and never sad.

Try hard as he might,

to be a good little tike.

Trouble seems to find him

no matter where he goes.

What's his latest adventure?

TRADITIONAL RHYMING POEMS & SHORT STORIES

nobody really knows.

A golf ball through the greenhouse roof

of the local florist shop.

Chief Biggs knocking on Diddley's door,

"This nonsense has to stop."

The sign clearly read, "Wet Cement,"

Of course, Diddley had to leave his foot print.

His dad said, "Son, you just don't understand,

how often your fun seems to get out of hand."

Your reputation precedes you for trouble, you know!

All the time, and wherever you go.

Curiosity I believe is where it begins.

No sooner free of one mess,

and it starts all over again.

Perhaps someday, Diddly will mature.

But for now, his future unsure.

You'll have to forgive me,

The animal shelter just called, said something about,

Well, seems Diddley just left the animals out.

WAYNE B. BOWMAN

TAKE MY ADVICE

I don't drink, and I don't smoke.

I like country music, and a good clean joke.

I work all day, and sleep all night.

So, me and my woman have no time to fight.

We been married nigh' on forty years.

Been a lot of laughs, and been a few tears.

We've seen the good, and we've seen the bad.

Been through some happy, and been through some sad.

If not for her, let me tell you son,

this old boy'd just be a bum.

Now, if I can give you one piece of advice.

Find yourself a girl that's sweet and nice.

Settle down and raise a family,

and the day will come that you will see

that you've created a history.

A story perhaps, someday to be told,

to your children's children when your gray and old.

Teach by example, is what I've said.

and, learn from these few words you've read.

Treat her well, try not to fight.

Kiss her on the cheek, and bid her goodnight.

Cause, if you know what's best son, she's always right.

THE FAN-ATTIC

I met a man that lives down the street from me,

who collects autographs you see.

Some, he pays for,

and some he gets for free.

Ernie's been collecting all his life,

long before he ever met his wife.

One day, I had an opportunity

when invited to his attic to see,

his prized assortment of curiosities'.

Sports items, movie props and clothing galore.

All with famous signatures

like Liz Taylors back stage door.

As I looked all around

at the things he had found

it soon became clear to me,

that this man's obsession

has become his profession

in gathering pieces of history.

WAYNE B. BOWMAN

Signatures of the rich and famous,

Roy Rogers, and Famous Amos.

I saw Elvis, Zoro and Andy Garcia,

Mickey Mantle, Karloff and Pancho Villa.

Martin and Lewis, and of course John Wayne,

James Arness, Lucy and Lois Lane.

Jackie Gleason, and Lassie, the dog

Tonto, Miss Piggy and Kermit the Frog.

Larry, Curly and Moe.

Orson Wells and Marlon Brando.

George Jones and Tammy Wynette,

Ozzie Nelson, and his wife Harriet.

Of course, David and Ricky

And a well-known mouse named Mickey.

A crooner named Bing,

a blues man named King.

Rose, Bench and DiMaggio,

And some long-haired dude named Fabio.

Mister "T," and Fibber McGee,

and Batty Hattie from Cincinnati.

Well, I could go on, but for now I'll stop.

Oh! There is one more that deserves a mention.

Old Barney, the famous Mayberry Cop.

TRADITIONAL RHYMING POEMS & SHORT STORIES

BUGS

Tiny creatures I cannot see,

cause me to suffer such allergies.

Ugly critters, oh my so small,

from head to toe is where they crawl.

What they're up to should be a crime.

Devouring my flesh one bite at a time.

And when they are done feasting on me,

I'll turn into dust and cease to be?

A nuisance of irritation they really deliver.

If it wasn't dust mites, It'd probably be chiggers.

Don't walk through the grass on a hot summer day,

or a nasty price you surely will pay.

Invisible spiders is what they are.

Take my advice and stay in the car.

Arachnids that burrow down into my skin.

Then they leave,---- but they'll be back again.

WAYNE B. BOWMAN

NAP TIME

Now, I'm not one to be nosey,

Or even care what others may think.

To eaves drop is just not my style,
No matter what anyone thinks.

She thinks that I'm sleeping,

but I'm really not you see.

So, little does she know,

it's all just a show,

cause I hear everything she says about me.

Each day around three or so,

I've gone as far as I can go.

No longer feeling my best,

I close my eyes to get some rest.

I feel better when I doze,

But as everyone knows,

That's not really news.

One always feels better after a snooze

TRADITIONAL RHYMING POEMS & SHORT STORIES

CHAPTER 2

ANYTHING GOES

A TIME OF REFLECTION

As he sits today, this lonely old man,

Memories flooding back, overwhelm him again.

Memories of a time not so long ago.

Seems almost like yesterday, you know.

Staring at a marker in front of him.

The name he sees, of a dear old friend.

Lost in a conflict they thought never to end.

One life lost, that another may live.

No greater gift can anyone give.

Truth is, this was a battle they could not win.

Upon returning, no hero's welcome did they receive.

Cursed and spat upon, so difficult to believe.

For many, the choice not theirs to make.

Still, they served valiantly, make no mistake.

"Should've been me," he says, wiping tears from his face.

"In a heartbeat you know, I would take his place."

"So, when my time comes, and it will someday you know,

remember this man who saved **my** life, a half century ago."

OLD DOC'

Well, old Doc wasn't the man he used to be,

so many years ago, you see.

Too many regrets, and too many tears.

And far, far too many years.

The bottle got the best of him,

again, and again, and again.

One cannot turn back time, he would say,

so, where I am is where I'll stay.

And know this, I'll always be your doctor.

I'll always be your friend,

but I'll always be just who I am

until the bitter end.

You can count on me, through thick and thin,

to be there when you need me,

no matter where I've been.

For it's my duty to serve, you see.

So, my friend, fear not.

I'm always at your beckon call,

giving it all I've got.

And when I'm gone,

I hope you'll remember me,

for not the man I became,

but the man I used to be.

WAYNE B. BOWMAN

I REMEMBER WHEN

I remember a time when life was simple,

so many years ago.

Longing now for those days of my youth.

Where, oh where did they go?

When candy was a penny,

gas at twenty-five cents.

Almost as cheap as a loaf of bread.

Now, did that really make any sense

I remember CB radios.

Just one thing more we thought would last.

Whitewall tires and fender skirts,

we thought were such a blast.

Frisbees, slinkies and pogo sticks.

A few of the ways we got our kicks.

Skate boards, stilts and scooters too.

Just to mention a very few.

When doctors would come to your home,

and you could run a tab at the general store.

And your hand shake was good enough for a loan.

Those days are gone, forever more.

If you had seen the things that I have,

you'd understand why I miss the past.

So many wonders of my youthful days

That I thought would surely last.

IT'S ABOUT TIME

They say, time is of the essence,

what-ever that means.

Important I suppose.

Often measured in timeless scenes.

The future is here and then it's gone.

Sort of a pause, but not for long.

It comes and it goes,

hours, seconds and micros.

It's the same for us all,

sixty marks, dashes or dots.

Days, months and years, that's it.

Then no more to be got.

But then, over and over, it all starts again.

So repetitious one might say,

if watching a clock eight hours a day.

Tick tock, tick tock, slowly slipping away.

They say our days are numbered.

I'd like to know mine if that's the case,

to live life to the fullest before leaving this crazy place.

Waiting for no one, rich or poor.

WAYNE B. BOWMAN

Weather you have or have not, it's the same old score.

Measured in so many ways.

Not really something one can save.

For if I could, to use once again,

I think I'd save it to use at the very end.

TRADITIONAL RHYMING POEMS & SHORT STORIES

WAYNE B. BOWMAN

MY HOME IN TENNESSEE

From atop this peak, a blanket of green I see.

Oh, how beautiful, and serene.

An eagle soars, so peaceful and free,

and all of this, is Tennessee.

Peaks of granite stretching for the sky,

towering pines a hundred feet high.

And the eagle flies.

Soon a rainbow of colors to appear,

as the tourist return, and fall draws near.

A landscape of red, orange, yellow and brown,

gently fluttering and drifting around.

Today, all is now covered in a first winter snow,

and again I stare at the beauty below.

And as the sun glistens on a pure sea of white,

my eyes once again stare in awe, at the eagle in flight.

As I turn and walk back through the snow,

my mind drifts to the future, for soon it will be spring,

when again the valleys burst forth,

and the birds begin to sing,

and once again the eagle will soar,

high above it all so majestic and free,

In this beautiful land I dearly love,

my home in Tennessee.

My home in Tennessee

STORMY DAY DREAMS

I love remembering my childhood yesterdays.

Fishing in the river, ice skating on the creek,

And those good old mountain ways.

Grandma and grandpa singing Gospel songs,

While my brothers and I tried to sing along.

But the one thing I will never forget,

is stretching out in the hay,

in that old red barn of grandpa's,

on a stormy summer day.

Starin' up at those massive beams,

holding it all up like Hercules.

Rain on that metal roof singing away.

Sounds of thunder, on a stormy summer day.

The steel roof rattles and the beams all shake.

The wind rolls down the valley,

and makes everything quake.

The clap of thunder is quaking,'

the old timbers are shaking.'

If it all comes down.

a new one we soon will be raising.

Now, the storms would come and go.

Then the mountains would glisten and glow.

And the creek would rise,

not at all a surprise,

and surely recede by tomorrow...

I remember so well,

that fresh washed smell,

that followed after the storm.

The valley now blanketed in a whisp of blue haze

Oh, how I long-- for those stormy summer days.

WAYNE B. BOWMAN

FACE IN THE MIRROR

Same thing every morning.

Such a pitiful site.

Mostly unsure if he was wrong or write.

Slowly opening one eye at a time,

Unable to make sense of reason or rhyme.

The face staring back at him,

lost and lonely, once again.

Hiding in a bottle has taken its toll,

destroying his body, devouring his soul.

Someday, maybe things will change.

Only the future to re-arrange.

Reliving a past, so painful you see.

Always the slave, never to be free.

Scars etched so very deep,

echo a promise he failed to keep.

Things that happened so long ago,

haunting him now and forever more.

Moments in time he'd like to forget,

scenes playing back in memory reset.

Visions of madness, suffering and pain,

driving him ever so slowly insane.

Terror unfolding before his eyes,

TRADITIONAL RHYMING POEMS & SHORT STORIES

watching his comrades dropping like flies.

"We will make it back, I promise!" he said.

The only one that didn't come back dead.

Wishing he had, but too late now.

Cursing the day, he made that vow.

WAYNE B. BOWMAN

THE WALL

We welcome people of other nations,

but only by legal expectations.

If that doesn't suite you,

then this you should know.

To the end of the line, or back to Mexico.

Now, someone said,

"I'll build a wall. Ten feet, twenty feet, thirty feet tall."

Well, let me tell you. That won't work at all.

Their determination I think I understand,

why they desperately try to escape their land.

They've had enough and can no longer cope,

in a dictatorship where there is no hope.

They seek freedom, peace and stability.

Now, that's okay, but do it legally.

Now, building a wall sounds like a plan,

but to get it done takes a real man.

A determined man who will take a stand,

and we don't have one of those right now.

The one we have wants to tear it down.

Now, if this issue really bothers you,

then there's only one thing that you can do.

Let's unite and present them with this demand.

To make that wall a hundred feet tall,

and extend it down the middle of the Rio Grande.

THE POET

Why does he fall asleep in the middle of day?
Awake most nights is what he'll say.
Can't sleep when it starts you know.
Unstoppable words with consistent flow.
Rolling along
like a newborn song.
Telling a story in rhythmic timing.
Orchestrated lyrics and melodic rhyming.
Like an artist creating with brushes and paint.
Some say it's art, some say it aint.
Taking liberty in word composition.
Moving them around to new positions.
Expressing himself the best way he knows,
with carefully constructed melodic prose.
Scarcely a subject that he won't tackle.
from storm fed rushing streams,
to campfires that snap and crackle.
First words on the page, often so few,
then taking a break, an attempt to renew.
Now thoughts once scattered,

come together with ease.

Once again flowing like a soft summer breeze.

Not trusting his memory, for surely, he'd blow it.

So goes the life, of the Waterfall Poet.

THE HUMMING BIRD

So fascinating to watch, this aerial ballet.

Fluttering about, then zipping away.

Light as a feather just hovering there.

Then gone in a flash like no time to spare.

How does he do it, I'd like to know.

So amazing it is, this phenomenal show.

Staring in awe of these tiny things.

Entranced by the blur of those delicate wings.

Ever so close their fluttering could be heard.

So is the sight and sound, of the tiny humming bird.

TRADITIONAL RHYMING POEMS & SHORT STORIES

HE'S A CRAFTSMAN

He knows he's blessed to be a craftsman,

with talents beyond compare.

Building things that he can use,

and some useful things to share.

Working on projects large and small.

Really doesn't matter, he loves them all.

Creating things so useful you see.

No thanks he often says, this ones on me.

Pieces of this and a little of that,

come together completely from scratch.

No sooner is one project finished,

in his mind a new one begins to hatch.

To see a vision in his head,

without a blue print to be read.

Hands and mind so synchronized,

come together to improvise.

Give him a hammer, nails and saw,

he'll build something that will amaze them all.

Someday he'll build a house you see,

a place to live for two or three.

All he needs is a piece of wood.

He'll turn it into something good.

WAYNE B. BOWMAN

Save the scraps, he'll use them later.

Maybe he'll build an elevator.

Sometimes hours, or maybe days.

He never ceases to amaze.

How much pleasure he derives,

that helps him mentally to survive.

If only he'd known years ago.

So much more he'd have to show.

Time squandered in his youth; you know.

Water under the bridge, or so it goes.

So, take heed my friend as it is given.

Don't waste your youth in senseless living.

Find your gifts that God has given.

Use them for His work as He see's fitting.

Such gifts so useful not only for you,

Intended for those around you too.

A godly purpose is what they're for.

Fix a neighbor's window, mend her door.

Jesus was a carpenter, and so I've read.

And by His words we shall be led.

Don't wait til' your old to figure it out.

Following His example, is what it's about.

TRADITIONAL RHYMING POEMS & SHORT STORIES

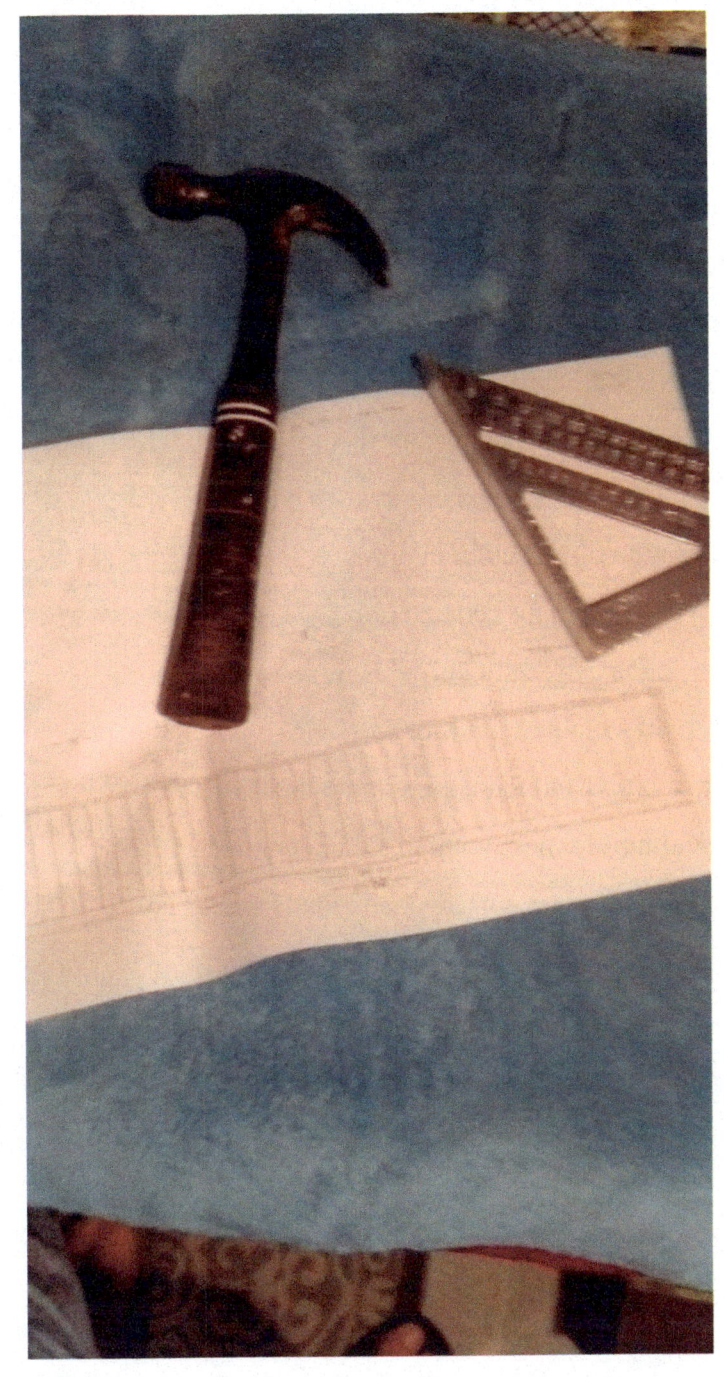

Tools of the trade.

WAYNE B. BOWMAN

THE EXPEDITION

Well, I really love my Ford Expedition.

It's a little old, but in great condition.

I bought it about a year ago.

It gets me to wherever I need to go.

It's an XLT, whatever that means.

Ruby Red Metallic is the color theme.

I love it man, but it's so hard to keep clean.

And a sand-colored cloth interior,

such a contrast to the red exterior.

This 5.4, she can really go.

Zero to 60 – eight seconds or so.

Three hundred and ten horses under the hood,

She's nothin' to mess with, that's understood.

Now - a work horse I needed, and that's what I got.

Just give it the gas and you're out like a shot.

Plenty of power when you need it the most.

Here, and then gone- like Casper the Ghost.

TRADITIONAL RHYMING POEMS & SHORT STORIES

THE GOOD ONES ARE ALL GONE

Seems like only yesterday,

before all the good ones went away.

A good laugh you could count for sure,

Ed Asner and Mary Tyler Moore.

Bud and Lou- always a good show,

right up there with Larry, Curly and Moe.

How about Stan and Ollie,

for some real laughs, by golly.

Laughter derived from good clean fun.

The Bowery Boys, always on the run.

Jackie and the Honeymooners, George and Gracie.

Their perfect timing always amazed me.

Bob Hope, for a really good show.

Especially for our troops at a USO.

No matter if over here, or over there.

Always getting there by land, sea or air.

Now, you may be too young

to know these praises that I've sung.

So, Google them if you will,

for a new found hysterical thrill.

Now where they are today,

I'd like to believe I can safely say.

They're all in heaven I know,

starring in one heck of a show.

WAYNE B. BOWMAN

WHO AM I?

I am the spirit of the un-born child.

Not even a name upon a file.

Deprived of a life I never will see.

Now God has my soul for eternity.

I am a spirit without earthly name.

Murdered you know, did they feel no shame?

An innocent life unable to feel,

the touch of a mother, so tender and real.

A mother so fearful of disgrace and scorn,

saw not God's value of this tiny un-born.

Deceived by her peers, now never to hear,

the gentle voice of one so dear.

No earthly joys am I able to give,

to those who deemed me unworthy to live.

I am the unheard voice of a weeping soul.

Once a life deemed worthless, you know.

In His eyes perfect and beautiful though.

I am a cry in the night that no one will hear.

A cry of innocence, not shame or fear.

Now far beyond the reach of man,

so truly loved by the Great I Am.

THE TROUBLE WITH KIDS TODAY

The trouble I see with kids today,

they just don't know how to go out and play.

Video games- texting- social media too,

Surely, they could find something better to do.

You know, back in my day

we couldn't wait to go out and play.

Socializing with others face to face,

just hanging out at our favorite place.

Pulling pranks, or sharing a joke,

over a milk shake or bottle of Coke.

A run through the sprinkler,

until our clothes are all soaked.

Hop scotch, skip rope and hide and seek.

Remember now, no fair if you peek.

Kick the Can, Hula Hoops and Pogo Sticks.

Bad Minton, Horse Shoes and magic tricks.

What's the matter with you?

Get up off of that couch.

Put down that phone,

and since when do you slouch.

Oh my, longing for a time so simple you see.

If only things could be like they used to be.

I suppose that's life, what else can I say.

Things will never again, be like yesterday.

WAYNE B. BOWMAN

THE OLD FIVE AND DIME

I remember the old FIVE AND DIME,

From so much a simpler time.

When any girl or boy,

could find endless joy,

just reading a book of rhyme.

They had toys galore,

from ceiling to floor.

Oh yes! And things for mom and dad too.

And on the way out, without a doubt,

some Double Bubble to chew.

Cracker Jacks, and penny candy you'd see,

which back then seemed almost free.

Bob-O-Links, Slinky Dinks and wind-up barking dogs,

Paddle Ball, paper dolls and a box of Lincoln Logs

Jacks, Yo-Yo's, Tidily Winks and Tinker Toys.

Wonderful childhood memories for grown up girls and boys.

Nickle, dime or quarter then.

Today worth a fortune, you know.

Oh! to be a kid again,

if back in time I could go.

To bring back as many as I could,

and put them all in an antique show.

TRADITIONAL RHYMING POEMS & SHORT STORIES

The old Five and Dime Store in St. Augustine Florida.

WAYNE B. BOWMAN

A VOICE IN THE NIGHT

I don't know where they come from

these crazy words you've read.

Seems like out of nowhere

they show up in my head.

Waking me up in the middle of night.

Hairs a mess, I must be a sight.

Sitting at the table typing out each word,

hoping someday, that this voice will be heard.

Inspiration, laughter, sorrow and pain.

Sometimes these words just drive me insane.

Haunting me every day you know,

following me everywhere I go.

Heaven forbid I go back to sleep,

for I know till morning, they just won't keep.

When I awake, they'd be gone for sure,

lost and forgotten forever more.

Can't afford to waste them, you know.

So, whenever they call, I just have to go.

I sit here now mostly half asleep,

Typing these words that I surely must keep.

Sometimes I'm blank, but not deterred,

for this voice cries out----

I just want to be heard.

ENOUGH IS ENOUGH

Well, I've had about enough of this nine to five.

Those fancy suites, white shirts and ties.

So, I told my boss I'm going out the door.

Won't be lookin" back, don't work here no more.

So sick and tired of this silly rat race.

I'm goin' crazy runnin' all over the place.

That's why I've had it clear up to here.

I think I've settled for the wrong career.

He said, now son I think I understand,

why you feel like a down trodined man.

You worked so hard for all these years,

with little to show cept" blood, sweat and tears.

So, I won't blame you if you leave this place

now that you've firmly stated your case.

Thought about it myself a time or two.

Just take some time to think it through.

You know life is tough and not always fair,

but I want you to know I really do care.

I know times are hard, and things are tight,

but trust in me, it'll soon be right.

So, I asked him, "Man, just what-a-ya' mean?"

"If I stay around here, nothins' gonna' change."

He said, "Son, you don't have a clue,

just what they're about to offer you.

Now, trust me when I say you've come into view,

with the higher ups, and yours truly too.

There ain't a job in this place that you can't do,

provided you really wanted to.

One of the smartest here, without a doubt.

Just taken them too long to figure that out.

So, I put in a word with the CEO,

and he said fine, let's see how far he can go.

So, starting Monday you're in charge of this floor.

You see son, it's not you that's walkin' out that door."

TRADITIONAL RHYMING POEMS & SHORT STORIES

THE OLD MAN FROM THE MOUNTAIN

The old man came down from the mountain,

to trade his furs for supplies.

Most were afraid.

Must have been those deep dark eyes.

Big as an old oak tree.

Ducks his head when he walks through the door,

Never said much, kinda' quiet for sure

Dropped his head again when leaving the store

Rawhide hat, and long hiking stick

A rifle on his horse,

A six gun on his hip.

Buck skin from head to toe.

Where he's from,

They really don't know.

Long jagged scar from chin to his eye.

I once asked, but he didn't reply.

Some say he fought a grizzly toe to toe

to save a small Indian child.

He won't admit it though.

It's said the Indians revere him as one of their own

and will protect him wherever he roams.

WAYNE B. BOWMAN

He once loved a squaw never to part.

She caught fever, and broke his heart.

They say his tears made the rivers overflow

and new one's flow where they never did go.

Indians call him, "Man who cried a river,"

As for the rest of us,

we'll probably never know.

The old man from the mountain died in 1892.

The Indians say his spirit still roams these mountains

ever watching over and protecting them.

You know, I think I'd like to believe that too.

TRADITIONAL RHYMING POEMS & SHORT STORIES

TRUCK DRIVER SURVIVER

Lord, I know I'm runnin' heavy tonight.

Been sleepin' all day, and on the road all night.

No matter my speed, fifty miles to the hour.

To many steep hills, and losin' power.

Black dog tryin' to take me to my grave.

I'm prayin" the Lord my soul to save.

Tryin' hard to keep it between the lines.

By-passin' scales; can't afford no fines.

Double clutchin, 'and jammin' those gears.

Losin'n control, my greatest fear.

Car behind me is way to close.

Can't even see him in that ole' west coast

White lines are just a flashin' by.

Makin' me dizzy, playin' tricks with my eyes.

The longer I drive, the more I find,

by the end of the day I'm still runnin' behind.

Five days on and three days home.

Time with my family, and then I'm gone.

Back on the road and all alone.

That's the way it goes when you drive a rig.

Just wish I had more time for the kids.

WAYNE B. BOWMAN

I think next month I'm gonna' retire.

Spend time with my family around a roaring campfire.

Well, it's finally here, and todays the day.

I'll turn in my keys and collect my pay.

Hello Sam.

How's retirement you say?

Just like on the road, my friend

Tryin' to make up for lost time every day.

TRADITIONAL RHYMING POEMS & SHORT STORIES

MISTER ENGINEER

Here comes old Engine number 49

rolling in as usual, right-on time.

Mister engineer, tell me where you've been.

Do you think you'll ever go back again?

Four times a month, you know I make this run,

From east to west just racin' the sun.

Three days out, and three days back.

I guess I'll always be ridin' this track.

Movin' those goods up and down the line.

For thirty years now puttin' in my time.

Sometimes more than eighty miles an hour.

Crankin' those diesels to maximum power.

I've seen a lot in my years on these rails.

From mountain tops to dessert trails.

I've seen wild mustangs and cowboys too.

Indians and bison, but very few.

If I had it to do all over again,

I suppose I'd be right where I am.

I like the sound of that diesels hum

roaring westward toward the setting sun.

Clickety clack, clickety clack all day long.

Nothin' like the sound of that endless song.

Haulin' gravel, pipe and lumber today.

WAYNE B. BOWMAN

Got loaders and dozers goin' back they say.

And I suppose when my time comes,

I'll be ridin' these rails into the setting sun.

And you know that's okay by me,

Cause there's no place else I'd rather be.

TRADITIONAL RHYMING POEMS & SHORT STORIES

CHAPTER 3

FROM THE HEART

THE LAST THING I SEE

When my time is gently fading away,

and the stars have lost their shine.

When there are no glowing sunsets,

to warm this heart of mine.

No more majestic mountains,

with sparkling waters that flow,

endlessly across stones and pebbles

to lush valleys far below.

No more laughing children playing in the park,

or dancing moon beams on the lake there in the dark.

No more dances in the moonlight.

No more walks along the shore.

How then shall I miss these cherished scenes,

when memory is no more?

So many memories throughout the years,

all of those that we have shared.

Not a one would I have tucked away,

had I not sincerely cared.

Now my eyes are slowly closing.

TRADITIONAL RHYMING POEMS & SHORT STORIES

Soon, there'll be no more to see,

but the love shining in those beautiful eyes

softly looking back at me.

Now, there are no more tomorrows

to look forward to today.

So, as I gaze into your eyes this one last time,

know my love, that this is what I pray.

Please bless me Lord in heaven,

with memory renewed,

of all these things of which I've spoken

and this love that I once knew.

But if there is but one, He says that I must choose.

Then know this my sweet love,

It would be my last memory of you.

WAYNE B. BOWMAN

NOT WHAT YOU EXPECTED

Whatever it is you think,

I should or should not be.

A disappointment I'm quite sure,

is what you must think of me.

Trying so hard to please,

all those I truly love.

Constantly praying for intervention

from the Father up above.

No matter how hard I try,

to succeed in things I do,

failures are ever so many,

successes, ever so few.

They say no one is perfect,

with this I must agree.

Now, one might even see,

a perfect example of that in me.

I try always to be so good,

but things sometimes turn out bad.

I always try to be happy,

and usually end up feeling sad.

But if there's one thing I truly know,

although sometimes fail to see,

is that somewhere in my future,

God has a perfect plan for me.

ONE MORE DAY

Lord, I know my time is here.

Things left undone my greatest fear.

So many things I need to say.

For one more day is what I pray.

Things I could have said throughout the years,

that would have dried so many tears.

Apologies without delay.

Lord, all I ask is one more day.

Another chance to say goodbye

to broken hearts that I've made cry.

To beg forgiveness for things I've done.

For all those battles I thought I'd won.

To mend fences that I've left broken

by words in anger that were spoken.

Oh, to only have the time it takes

to say I'm sorry for my mistakes.

Knowing now that I was wrong,

allowing pride to be so strong.

For my time is now, but Lord I pray.

If only I'd known this yesterday.

Then, if this were yesterday I could say;

"Thank you Lord, for one more day."

DOES IT REALLY MATTER ANYMORE?

Does it really matter anymore

if the sun doesn't rise,

or descend below the evening skies?

Does it really matter if tomorrow

he doesn't open his eyes?

Will the pain just wash away

all the guilt of yesterdays?

So little time one has.,

how soon it slips away.

Each day he awakes, to silence.

But the silence is deafening to his ears.

No more "good morning my love.

How are you today?"

Facing each new day, his greatest fear.

Will time simply erase

all the terrible mistakes,

or the memories there of,

and bring back the glow

that together they once knew

of that precious and forever true love?

TRADITIONAL RHYMING POEMS & SHORT STORIES

THINKING OF YOU

I passed a flower shop today,

In the window were pretty bouquets.

I thought of you.

Saw a couple walking the beach today,

holding hands along their way.

and I thought of you.

Sitting in the front porch swing,

the crickets still chirp, the birds still sing,

and I think of you.

Sitting on a park bench, on a bright summer day,

watching the squirrels and the children play.

while thinking of you.

The sound of a church choir on a Sunday morn,'

a young couple playing with their tiny newborn.

I think of you.

Tree frogs singing down by the creek,

a handful of memories of which I speak.

And I think of you.

I think of you so often, sweet memories so dear,

of days long ago, when I held you near.

You're gone now, but no matter what I do,

thanks to those memories,

you're still here with me, -----

and I'm still thinking of you.

THE OLD GUITAR

On the wall in his den hangs an old guitar,

from which sweet melodies once did flow.

A Martin acoustic, one of the best by far.

Silent now for many years you know.

In the hallows of his mind he can still hear,

House of Gold- and I Saw the Light.

That old guitar resonating so clear,

as his dad played and sang every Saturday night.

At eighty-three a stroke took away,

once and for all his ability to play.

No more Near My God to Thee,

Blessed Assurance- or Love lifted me.

Though, who knows, perhaps some day

that old Martin guitar may once again play,

Wildwood Flower, Victory in Jesus

or, Down to The River to Pray.

But for now- he'll leave things just as they are,

to remind him of that man he once knew

whenever he looks, at that old guitar.

TRADITIONAL RHYMING POEMS & SHORT STORIES

Dad's Martin Guitar.

WAYNE B. BOWMAN

MEMORIES

I think of days gone by, from time to time.

Bits and pieces that cross my mind.

Fleeting moments tucked away, inside my head,

like words on a page someday to be read.

Memory, sometimes it works for you,

but far too often those times are few.

You know what I'm talking about, I'm sure.

Affecting us all, young, old, rich or poor.

Little things so important someday to recall.

Trivial things easy, and priorities not at all.

Memories, so valuable as can be.

Enjoy them now before they flee.

Living in the past is all I live for.

If only I knew how to re-open that door.

A treasure trove of days gone by.

Fleeting pictures on the fly.

To be re-lived is what they cry,

but not that simple, I don't know why.

Images of things that I once knew,

ever so slowly fading from view.

Places I know that I have been,

to soon, never to be seen again.

Beautiful sunsets beyond compare.

TRADITIONAL RHYMING POEMS & SHORT STORIES

Words of love no other can share.

Things I used to love to recall,

Now such a struggle, to remember at all.

I'm an old man now, so heed what I say.

Take lots of pictures and store them away.

Tell family and friends where they might be,

so later on, once again you may see,

those tiny slices of memory bliss.

A silent glance, a loved one's kiss.

So, write things down, that's all I'll say,

rely not on memory, be led not astray.

So, here's the question that I must ask.

Could it simply be – we never were meant to relive the past.

WAYNE B. BOWMAN

BLINK OF AN EYE

What is life, but the blink of an eye.

A time to laugh, a time to cry.

Much too short we sometimes say.

Collecting those memories along the way.

Looking back at days now gone.

Fondly remembering each and every one.

Taking the time to savor a few,

first and foremost, those memories of you.

Like pictures in an album,

preserved for posterity,

lingering most on the ones of you and me.

Sharing them with those I love,

a painted picture for them to see.

Recollections, to me so dear,

fearful someday they'll all disappear.

Now if that day comes,

and the glimmer in my eyes should go away,

and the voice you once heard, now has nothing to say,

Gaze deep into those eyes,

for I want you to know,

that I'm reliving those memories of so long ago.

For you, so difficult to understand,

But know this, my darling.

I'm really quite happy, just where I am.

THE LISTENER

Library- grocery or Doctors office.
Makes no difference to them.
Most would think a one-time encounter.
But she knows, she'll see them again.
Without them even knowing it,
they've made a brand-new friend.
They'll remember her as the one who listens,
when no one else seems to care.
Always willing, to lend an ear,
and the promise of a heart felt prayer.
At ninety-two, so small and frail,
one they could count on to listen without fail.
Total strangers, so often it would be,
seeking not to be judged or condemned.
So, she would listen, and always for free.
Many baring their souls, just for her to hear.
Divorce, cancer, the wayward and the lost.
Stories of cheating, hatred and fear,
and life changing mistakes, at such a great cost.
When they were through talking

she'd look at them and say,

"Just know that God loves you

and hears you when you pray."

If you asked her why she bothers,

her response would simply be,

"Sometimes a soul just needs someone to listen."

Someone like you or me."

She's been gone for some time now,

and you know I really miss her.

For when God made my mother,

He blessed her to be,

a really good listener.

TRADITIONAL RHYMING POEMS & SHORT STORIES

THE OLD WOODSHOP

Standing in the doorway of this old woodshop.

Stone cold silence is all I now hear,

where the sounds of machinery once made itself clear.

Now so cold and empty.

No sound of a saw or drill to be heard.

No tap- tap- tap of a hammer,

creating feeders for the birds.

Hand tools once shiny and spotless you know,

precisely organized and ready to go.

Each placed on a shelf side by side,

Chisels, gauges and a metric slide.

Rusty now, so unlike before.

I can almost sense his presence,

as I stand here just inside the old woodshop door.

Each tool I touch, I feel his hand holding mine,

as if guiding and teaching me for the very first time.

Dusty bird feeders and flag boxes sitting about.

It'll take forever to sort it all out.

If he were here now, I feel certain he would say,

"You can't keep it all son, so give some away.

Let other craftsmen make use of these things,

building bird houses, feeders and front porch swings."

Now I step outside, and glance back once more.

WAYNE B. BOWMAN

Oh, what wonderful memories all locked up
just beyond my daddy's old woodshop door.

TRADITIONAL RHYMING POEMS & SHORT STORIES

CHAPTER 4

FROM THE SOUL

THE WHISPER

Sometimes, in the middle of night,

when all seems well, silent and right.

At times he will hear,

a gentle whisper in his ear.

Is he awake, or is this a dream?

Suddenly, more real than it might seem.

An assuring voice ever so clear.

One of love, not one to fear.

Words of advice, not to be ignored.

Far better than others he's explored.

Encouragement, when he's beaten down.

A ray of hope when there's none to be found.

A little rebuke when it's needed most,

straight from the heart of the Holy Ghost.

Directions to where he needs to be.

Always for the best, he soon will see.

No better counselor anywhere to be found.

Ever listening for His gentle, and comforting sound.

Middle of day, or middle of night.

WAYNE B. BOWMAN

He knows when it feels just right,

and so, he listens-- for the whisper.

ROSES and THORNS

Life is full of roses and thorns.

Sometimes we're forced to face the storms.

Fighting head on relentlessly.

Determined to win, not to concede.

Pain and sorrow, evil and despair,

beating us down, not always fair

Free yourself from the thorns.

Go to Him in prayer.

Then, a visit from a friend puts a smile on your face.

Words of comfort, and a loving embrace.

The smile of a stranger holding a door,

can melt away sadness like never before.

Such is life in its various forms.

And now you know what I mean, by roses and thorns

TRADITIONAL RHYMING POEMS & SHORT STORIES

Clipped from moms rose bush after her tragic death in 2019. The bush it came from at one time towered to eight feet in height. She was so proud of it.

WAYNE B. BOWMAN

THE OTHER SIDE OF LIFE

On the other side of life,

as we stand before the Son,

when there are no more tomorrows,

and yesterdays are gone,

remember this, one life is all it took,

a life beyond compare,

to free the world from the slavery

of Satan's deadly snare.

He gave His life so long ago

that all mankind might see,

the depth to which the Father's love might go

to rescue you and me.

Never more can Satan own us,

though tempt us, that he may.

Bought with the blood of Jesus,

for eternity and a day.

So, maybe now you understand

these words that I now say.

There is a life here after, as he promised it to be.

A bounty of joy, peace and love,

For all eternity.

TRADITIONAL RHYMING POEMS & SHORT STORIES

I AM BLESSED

I am blessed my God should love me so,

to give His one and only Son.

To know my every daily need,

and provide for each and every one.

I am blessed He loves me when I am weak,

and encourages me when I am strong.

To lift me up when I may fall,

to rebuke me when I am wrong.

To hear my plea each time I pray,

and grant me grace along the way.

He says to me, "I am here."

whispering softly in my ear.

I am blessed He sees me in my despair,

at times when life may not be fair.

That's when He shows me signs you see,

and takes me where He wants me to be.

Day in and day out the troubles I face,

will pale in comparison to His saving grace.

No matter that I may falter,

I'll always try my best.

For this one thing I'll always know,

I am truly blessed.

WAYNE B. BOWMAN

WHEN WILL I LEARN?

OH! How I struggle each day,

with plans so foolishly made.

My brains up to its old tricks again.

Same old, same old. What can I say?

Self-appointed you see,

to carry things through.

But, why must it always be me,

when I should turn it all over to you.

Short term and long-term goals I make.

When will I ever learn, not to make that mistake?

Aware quite well, I need to break that spell,

and put God in control, for heaven's sake.

WHEN MY TIME HAS COME

When my time has come, and life fades away.

As darkness surrounds me on that fateful day.

In that final hour, I'll not be afraid.

I know heaven awaits me, for my debt has been paid.

When I have crossed over to eternity's light,

joining friends and loved ones.

What a beautiful sight.

Fear not my darling, weep not for me.

Take comfort in knowing that I am now free.

Mere moments in time, so precious and few.

Waste not even one, for they never renew.

Once faded away, cannot be retrieved.

Gone now forever, so be not deceived.

My race is over, what more can I say.

Worry not for tomorrow, make the best of today.

WAYNE B. BOWMAN

WHEN THINGS COME UNDONE

When things just seem to come undone,

and the answer isn't always clear.

Just take your burdens to the Lord,

and He will calm your fear.

Almighty God, I think you know,

is in control, so just let it go.

He has a plan so I am told,

To keep you safe within His fold.

Don't let it overwhelm you, set all your fears aside.

Open the door to your heart, and allow Jesus to reside.

He'll be there when you need Him, to help you find your way.

Keep your eyes upon the prize, being careful not to stray.

Now, if you follow this advice, and remember what I say,

so very soon you'll start to see, your stress and worries fade away.

So now I think that you can see,

what the answer will always be.

There is only one you know,

and I'll say it again before I go.

So, let this be my final refrain.

Be it known throughout the earth

Jesus is His name.

WALK ON THE WATER

Just walk on the water.

Take a leap of faith.

Get out of the boat, and don't be afraid.

When life overwhelms you, and you think it's the end.

Just reach out to Jesus when you need a friend.

Trust in Him for he is the way.

He'll love and guide you safely over the waves.

From time to time,

it will surely be rough.

Just trusting in Him is more than enough.

When the waves are so high, and the water so deep.

He is the answer. It's Him that you need.

When life overwhelms you, just reach out to Him.

He is waiting to hear, that you need a friend.

So, trust in Jesus all along the way,

and know that He hears you, what more can I say.

If you think for a moment that this is not true.

Go to Him in prayer, and He will come through.

It may not be the answer you were hoping for.

Could be God's way of opening a new door.

So, just walk on the water.

HE WILL LEAD THE WAY

Just give your life to Christ,

and He will lead the way.

For he has paid the price,

so, turn to Him today.

He'll turn your life around.

No longer are you lost.

You now have been found.

For He has paid the cost.

The price of your salvation,

can never be repaid.

All He asks is dedication,

for you truly have been saved.

Lead your sisters and your brothers.

Tell them the Good News too.

They in turn will lead others,

so many souls shall be renewed.

Just give your life to Christ,

and He will lead the way.

For your sins He paid the price,

so, turn to Him today.

Any time you have some doubt,

just go to Him in prayer.

Then He will sort things out.

As promised, He's always there.

Trials and troubles you may find,

as you walk along your way.

Just keep your eyes on Jesus,

and he will tell you what to say.

So, just give your life to Christ,

and He will lead the way.

For your sins He paid the price,

so, give your life to Christ.

WAYNE B. BOWMAN

THE ANSWER

So many friends and family have past beyond my door,

to a place where pain and suffering will trouble them no more.

To wonders far beyond this world's heartaches and its strife.

Walking the streets of heaven now blessed with eternal life.

Storms will come and storms will go.

Don't ask me to explain.

Reach out when all seems lost,

calling on Jesus, for that's His name.

When you sometimes think no one can hear,

so all alone and so much fear.

Often, more than you can bare.

When you need Him most, He's always there.

Take heart my friend in what I say.

When all seems hopeless, He will lead the way.

TRADITIONAL RHYMING POEMS & SHORT STORIES

THE TRUE MEANING of CHRISTMAS

Christmas is that time of year,

when we think of loved ones far and near

to share our gifts and holiday cheer.

Ornaments on a tree so shiny and bright.

Glittering tinsel and sparkling blue lights.

Pretty bows on gifts tucked under a tree.

Some gifts for you, and maybe one for me.

It's Santa this, and Santa that.

A jolly fat man in a red and white hat.

The spirit of Christmas is in giving, you see.

Tis, more blessed to give than it is to receive.

Now, Santa brings joy to many, even I must agree.

But there's one gift even Santa can't bring.

That's salvation for you and for me.

I'll tell you a story maybe you've heard before,

of this child of God who would even the score.

The ultimate sacrifice is what it would take

to right the wrongs and clear the slate.

He came to earth as savior of man.

Born of a virgin, from the Great I Am.

Sent here to save us as prophesied.

Thirty-three years He lived, then died.

WAYNE B. BOWMAN

He died for us upon that tree.

And now that you've heard, I hope you'll agree,

His life once given has set us free.

There were no decorations so tiny and bright.

Not even a song of winter delight.

Only sadness, grief and despair,

then freedom for all to share.

From humble and peaceful beginnings,

to a cruel and tragic end.

His mission on earth now finished,

for us to reap the dividend.

The debt is paid, you are free to go.

The gates of heaven now open.

Once closed by sin, you know.

Hope now you know and have figured it out,

Christ is what Christmas is really about.

TRADITIONAL RHYMING POEMS & SHORT STORIES

MORNING PRAYERS

Each morning as I rise,

I thank God for making me wise.

Thanking Him for all the things I love,

knowing so well, they're on loan from above.

Thanking Him for all those in my life,

my faithful friends, my loving wife.

People I've met along the way.

Those that taught me how to pray,

and not hate those that offend me so.

Turn the other cheek, and just let it go.

Grateful for my time He gave,

watching it follow me to the grave.

Devouring it one breath at a time,

knowing so well, it's not really mine.

Present gone too soon, never to return.

The future now, my only concern.

For the trail behind cannot be changed,

only the future re-arranged.

So, each morning as you rise,

ask the Lord to make you wise.

Ask Him for all the time He may give,

and that others see wisdom in the way you live.

WAYNE B. BOWMAN

That you may show love to those you meet,

in your church and on the street.

Thank Him for all of these you have read,

and so many more I've yet to have said.

So, in closing I thank Him for the Son He gave,

And the forgiveness that follows me to the grave.

Thank you, Lord, for everything.

WHAT WOULD YOU DO IF---?

What would you do if you saw a man,

looking for food in a garbage can?

Would you turn your back and walk away?

or show him love and extend a hand.

What would you do if you saw him sleeping,

on a park bench all covered in snow?

Would you walk on by,

or stop and try,

to find him a warm place to go?

What would you do if you heard from a little bird,

that the lady next door couldn't pay her rent?

A disabled child with huge medical expense

is where most of her money has went.

So, would you walk away?

or to the landlord and say,

I think I'd like to cover her rent.

What would you do if there was a knock at your door,

from a man that had no place else to go.

His cars broke down,

he's in a strange town,

and everything is buried in snow.

Would you send him away?

or invite him to stay.

WAYNE B. BOWMAN

And drive him for help tomorrow.

What would you do, if Jesus came back today?

Would you be ready for judgement?

Or would there be hell to pay?

TRADITIONAL RHYMING POEMS & SHORT STORIES

A BETTER PLACE

As you travel down this road of life,

pray daily to the Lord,

and I promise you will find.

His love so re-assuring, will give you peace of mind.

They beat Him and cursed Him, then nailed Him to a tree.

This agony alone it took, to save and set us free.

His life upon this earth, full of ridicule and scorn.

Still, He left this world a better place,

then it was when He was born.

All this He endured for the likes of you and me.

A pure and perfect sacrifice,

died, then risen for all to see.

Our sinful life now washed away,

a new one has begun.

Sanctified through the blood of Christ,

Gods one and only Son.

So, as you travel through this life,

full of hatred, sin and scorn,

try to leave this world a better place,

then it was when you were born.

WAYNE B. BOWMAN
MY BEST ADVICE

I've been down, and I've been out.

I've done with, and done without.

I've felt sadness and I've felt pain,

the hopelessness of going slowly insane.

The anguish of losing a loved one,

yet, knowing in my heart I must go on.

Lost and lonely, in my despair,

finding little comfort from those who care.

I've been right and I've been wrong.

I've been lost for way too long.

When I fall down as things get tough,

He comes along and picks me up.

He'll dust me off and send me on my way.

That's how I know he hears me when I pray.

Oh, how I wish everyone could see,

how He never fails to rescue me.

So, trust me in what I say.

Talk to Him, each and every day.

When things are good, and when they're bad.

When you're happy, and when you're sad.

Trust in Him, for His love is true,

and honor Him in all you do.

TRADITIONAL RHYMING POEMS & SHORT STORIES

CHAPTER 5

POETIC SHORT STORIES

THE FRONT PORCH SWING

On a good day, there he would be,

resting on his front porch swing.

Newspaper in one hand,

in the other, a steaming cup of tea.

A rather small man with snowy white hair.

So small, one might not even see him there.

A stream of gray smoke wafting from his pipe,

that lay next to him on a small wooden stand,

and a supply of Prince Albert there in a can.

Often seen walking in the rain,

by the church, firehouse or the old police station.

Sometimes by the depot staring at a train,

as if waiting for someone special.

Old red umbrella, and a red carnation.

"She used to love walking and laughing in the rain."

That's all he would say, except, "her favorite color was red."

"And she liked carnations" is what he once said

TRADITIONAL RHYMING POEMS & SHORT STORIES

I moved to Maggie Valley five years ago.

Seems Henri was the only person I'd get to know.

For hours we talked on that front porch swing.
Local news, politics, just about anything.
One neighbor said she thought he had a sister.

"Forty-five years is a lifetime."
he would say in almost a whisper.

I felt there was something he wasn't telling me,
but never asked respectfully.

As the years went by, it almost seemed
he wanted to hear more about my history.
He had worked a variety of jobs in the day
Car salesman, and part time stint on Broadway.

I went to see him for one last time today.
Flowers lined the front hall.
A red umbrella, and fedora hung on the wall.
He looked so at peace just lying there.
Black suit, red tie and a red carnation in his lapel.
Looking so distinguished with his snowy white hair.

A gentle smile upon his face,

As I stood there gazing, as if into space.

A woman in black approached

and gently wiped a tear from my face.

As if she knew me, which I thought somewhat odd.

"You must be Conner." she said, with a soft sort of smile.

"That I am." I replied with a nod,

and then stepped out of single file.

"I'm Lizzie, Henri's daughter."

"Oh! I'm sorry, He never said he had a child."

"Just one." She replied- "That's me."

"Let's step outside for a while.

Someplace where we can speak freely.

 Not surprised he never mentioned me.

We'd not spoken in years- you see.

Until a month or so ago that is,"- she said.

As we sat down on that old porch swing

she began telling me about personal things.

Somethings that happened so far in the past.

You know, mistakes with guilt that forever last.

Harsh words so hastily spoken,

so many promises, mostly broken

"At twenty, I left home for good.

An angry young woman with all the answers.

I'd make it on my own, or so I thought I could."

"It eventually started eating away at my heart.

Then about a month ago a friend of mine, --

you know, one of those close ones you share your feelings with

from time to time.

She gave me a poem titled "One More Day."

"The author signed his work- The Waterfall Poet.

His words forever changed me, but he'll never know it."

"It's about this man who is dying.

Such a terrible life, and he knows it.

And in his final hour he's pleading with God

for just one more day"

"He speaks of allowing pride to rule his heart.

He's not asking for a brand-new start.

Just the time to right the wrongs he has done.

Things ever since he's been running from.

WAYNE B. BOWMAN

To take back pain inflicted on those he loved.

That's what he pleads for, from his god above.

Time to make amends and beg for grace.

Frantically now, he pleads his case."

"This poem literally ripped my heart out.

Tore at my soul, and made me see

what forgiveness is all about."

"Like- like this poet- this total stranger was speaking directly to me.

This frightened me so, I must say.

That man never got his one more day."

"I was left sobbing my heart out.

I can't end up like him, I said with a shout."

"How much pain I must have caused him all those years.

Without a doubt, far too many tears."

"So, I took a chance and called him.

Would he even accept, my apology?

So afraid he wouldn't forgive me.

Would he hang up, I had to see."

"So, what happened? "I asked.

"Did he forgive you the past?"

--- "Like the story of the prodigal son,

he poured out his heart and said, "The past is done!"
"I had been such a fool, so selfish and proud,
granted way more grace than I should be allowed."

"So, I told him I'd come to visit, you see.
Oh, how little did I know it just wasn't to be."

"How sad, I said. So sorry it didn't happen."

"Me too." she replied.
"But I'll always be grateful for that one more day."

"I suppose I'll be moving into the old house." she said.
"Looks like we'll be neighbors Conner."

"Welcome to the neighborhood." I replied,
and nodded my head."

"Would you stop by once I'm settled in?
I'd like to hear what you know about him.
I've lost so many years, you know,
and at this point have nothing to show."

"I see you have his red umbrella, I said!
How often I would see him walking in the rain with it."

She began to cry, leaning herself against my shoulder.

"I'm sorry." I said, "I know it was your mothers, wasn't it?"

"Forgive me," she said. "Just a rush of memories coming back."

"I never really knew my mother; you see for she died when I was only three."

"Father brought me carnations and this umbrella of red

for me one day as I lay crying in my bed."

I just looked at her without saying a thing,

as I sat there speechless, on that front porch swing.

TRADITIONAL RHYMING POEMS & SHORT STORIES

THE LAST SUNSET

He wasn't a very big man.

Rather slight of build and somewhat tan.

About five foot four I would say.

Face etched with the scars of yesterday.

Each line a life story penned, as if upon a page.

Every Saturday evening you'd see him there,

with his funny little hat and cane

dancing all around the square.

Cane outstretched, held in both hands,

as if holding an invisible partner, and he would dance.

Around and around the tree's he would go.

People would watch as he put on a show.

One day I stopped to watch as he danced all around.

Gliding back and forth, scarcely touching the ground.

Fascinated for sure, I needed to know.

To inquire of his story, or should I let it go.

To chance such a dare, would he think me to bold.

Or would he think it an honor his story be told.

I went over and sat on a bench that was there,

and noticed his eyes had caught my stare.

And then on the bench beside me I saw,

a bouquet of flowers arranged so delicately

And suddenly I began to see,

precisely why he was watching me.

As his dancing subsided and came to an end,
he walked slowly toward me and said,
 "Good evening my friend."
"Mind if I sit with you?"

"No," I replied," "No, not at all."

So, he picked up the bouquet and sat down next to me.

"Catching your wind, I said, as I looked over to see."

"Well, you know, I'm not as young as I used to be."
"I can see, he said, by the look in your eyes,
you wonder why I do this, and not to my surprise."
"If you have the time, he said,
I'll be happy to fill you in,
and prove to you this old man isn't out of his head."

"I would love to hear, if you have time to tell."

He replied, "I do." and promised to tell it well.

So, I leaned back to get comfortable,

to take in every word of what would soon become

the greatest love story I'd ever heard.

He began—

I'm going to take you back to 1943.

A wounded soldier returning home,

wheeled across this park by his best friend you see.

When his eyes fell upon the most beautiful young girl.

Set his heart in a flutter, his mind in a whirl.

So lovely was she, selling flowers from a cart.

"Push me closer," I said, "for I must see

this vision of loveliness that has stolen my heart."

As they moved so much closer, so better to see,

to his friend he exclaimed, "This girl will someday marry me!"

"Push me closer," I said- "and lend me a dollar,

so, I may buy this love of my heart

a beautiful bouquet of flowers.

She was seventeen, and he was twenty- three.

From that day forward on this very square

they would dance so free.

As time went on, they would make their plans

until one day when she didn't show.

He waited until long past dark,

then off to her home fast as he could go.

He stayed with her until the end.

His broken heart never to mend.

Though a promise was made he would never forget.

"I'll dance for you darling until the final sunset."

"So now you know the story.

I dance to feel her once again in my arms.

The gentle warmth of her cheek against mine.

Some might say, reliving the glory.

The flowers, those are in memory of her.

I leave them here for all to see,

or any to take should it bring them a memory."

"Crazy! Perhaps, we'll see."

"I'm one hundred and two this Friday,

and as happy as I was in 43."

"So, as long as I am able you see,

I'll go on dancing every Saturday,

for Miss Laura Lee."

TRADITIONAL RHYMING POEMS & SHORT STORIES

AN OLD RUSTY FORD

Just an old rusty Ford,

A part of a history so sweet,

appeared on a trailer just down the street.

Chained to the frame as tight as could be,

awaiting someone with vision to come set it free.

So many holes ever here and there.

Some so large, seamed beyond repair.

A forty-nine coupe, once a beautiful site.

More or less now, just a horrible fright.

He must have a closer look and try to see,

if this ancient creation could new again be.

As he moves in close with pen and pad,

to see such decay made him somewhat sad.

Broken glass and all tires flat.

Springs poking through where a driver once sat.

One fender with holes between the dents.

A rusty front bumper all crooked and bent.

Overall condition, far from even fair.

A flat head V-8 made him stop and stare.

Breathless, he stood unable to speak.

Fascination from within beginning to peek.

"I must find the owner.

Is it even for sale?
Or just a rusty old loner."
What he saw next turned him two shades of pale.
A state trooper walking toward him with a curious look.
Stopping at the hitch he props up his foot.

"Isn't she a beauty?" he says, with a sly sort of grin.
"I sure would like to see her running again.
I just stopped by to hang a sign.
Used to be my gramp's, but now she's mine."

"How much are you asking for this bucket of rust?"

"Twelve hundred and it's yours.
No charge for the dust."

"My, such a number! the young man said,
Surely you are kidding."

"No, I assure you son, I'm not out of my head.
That's my starting number, how much are you bidding."

"Oh! Good grief, there's more air than metal.

TRADITIONAL RHYMING POEMS & SHORT STORIES

Now shall we discuss

the market value of rust?

I believe three hundred is where we should settle."

"Now, seriously I say,

you're suggesting I give it away.

I know your visions the same as my dream,

to make her once again polished,

all shiny and clean.

To hear that flat head rumble and roar,

as you drive through the mountains,

up and down the shore."

"This was my grandpa's car many years ago.

So, I'll tell you a story,

One I think you should know.

This car has history, for you see,

It once hauled shine from Maggie Valley to Tennessee."

"He bought it in Greenville I believe he said,

and told me the original color was red.

He repainted it flat black,

in the old shed out back.

He beefed up the rear springs you see,

for it was Gramp's who ran to Tennessee."

"He never was caught you know,

But told my daddy after his final run.

Can't afford to get caught by my own grandson."

"So, you see son, it would mean a lot to me,

to see it once again as it used to be."

"So, here's what I say.

Six hundred, and once it's restored,

you'll take me a ride in that forty-nine Ford.

Maybe a trip up to Tennessee

to bring back memories of my grandpa' and me."

So, what-a-ya say, do we have a deal?

I know you won't pass up such a good steal."

"I accept your deal,

with just one question," the young man said.

"When this old rusty Ford is fully restored,

should I paint it black, or should I paint it red?"

TRADITIONAL RHYMING POEMS & SHORT STORIES

THE MAN FROM TENNESSEE

So many memories,

praying so that they last.

We were just kids back then.

Precious memories from the past.

Without a doubt, my very best friend.

Even then, a head taller than me,

as we carved our initials in that old oak tree.

Swimming in the river on a hot summer day.

"Race you to the other side," he would often say.

Climbing in that old oak tree.

My best friend, Jake and me.

Nothing else mattered, cept' havin' fun.

Sharing dreams of someday following the sun.

I remember when he said, "Someday I'll travel to Mexico.

Oh, how I miss those days so long ago.

Target practice, with that old forty-five.

He'd hit the target every time.

At sixteen he could out draw any man alive,

Jake was my very best friend.

He knew he could count on me,

and I could count on him.

    Then one day, he just up and moved away.

WAYNE B. BOWMAN

Way out west somewhere, he intended to stay.

Not sure where, he didn't really say.

Sent me a letter when he'd settled in.

Stayin' in a dump called the DEW DROP INN.

Then he wrote me again back in eighty-six.

Got a job as Sheriff in a town called Blue Creek.

Built quite a reputation with a gun.

Detoured many an outlaw on the run.

He'd send me a letter once or twice a year,

and I'd let him know how things where back here.

Made the trip out to visit him some time ago.

Seamed the years had begun to take a toll.

Said he'd been hit several times,

But healed up just fine.

Said; "Being Sheriff ain't no easy job.

Don't know what makes a man wanna' kill and rob.

Desperation I suppose," he would say.

"Times bein" hard, maybe so."

Said, "Someday, one way or another I'll retire you know.

Maybe buy me a little place down in Mexico."

We sat and talked about the good old ways.

Fishin,' huntin' the old oak tree and those lazy days.

Sittin' in the shade neath' that old oak tree,

Jake, Loco the dog, and me.

Reminiscing and wondering now,

where did the years go.

Well, he's finally retired,

but he never made it to Ole' Mexico.

"But at least he made it back home, someone said.

Found himself a more permanent place to lay his head."

He's resting now, neath' that old oak tree,

And, yes, it's true, he's back in Tennessee.

It took a bullet in the back to bring him home,

to these mountains that he once did roam.

My head so full of sweet memories,

though my heart, so very sad.

As I gaze upon two stones next to his.

One marked "MOM," the other one, "DAD".

His stone simply reads;

JACOB ISAAC MORGAN, 1837 – 1893

Someday soon I will join them, in the shade of that old oak tree.

Mom, dad-- and brother Jake,

The Man from Tennessee.

Jake's Colt side arm

TRADITIONAL RHYMING POEMS & SHORT STORIES

THE BEGINNING AND THE END

I've had a rough life,

But now it's time to go.

I've been in the crowd,

I've been the star of the show.

At thirteen I ran away from foster care.

Said I've had enough.

They don't really care.

Ever since the day I stole that gun,

I've been a blight on society.

A man on the run.

So, I sit here now in this cold dark cell,

wondering, who do I blame

for this personal hell?

When I pulled the trigger

that took his life,

I didn't know he had a kid and a wife.

What a fool I've been.

Don't feel sorry for me.

This is what I deserve.

Guess I'll never be free.

That's my story.

Don't do what I've done.

and waste your life

as a man on the run.

Tomorrow they'll decide,

If I'm to live or die.

You need to go now.

Don't want you to see me cry.

There is no excuse for what I've done.

Done out of anger,

and not for fun.

Now, those are the facts from the very start,

lots of regrets and broken hearts.

Too many bridges to try to mend,

and that's the story of my life,

from beginning to end.

TRADITIONAL RHYMING POEMS & SHORT STORIES

THE OLD JUNK MAN

When I was just a little boy,
I remember a very special toy.
A cranking device I played with every day.
Given to me by an old man that lived down the road.
I thanked him many times for that delightful toy.

"Thanks for visiting me today.
I'm so happy it brought you joy."

Everyone called him the old junk man.
He'd just laugh and say he didn't mind.
"I'm much smarter than they think I am.
You see, I can make a buck on anything I find."

Sixteen buildings, so much to see.
I remember when he moved here from Tennessee.
He'd work throughout the night and into the day.
Putting up buildings to store things away.
Strange crooked lamps, a funny metal toy.
All kinds of treasures
to fascinate a ten-year-old boy.
Gizmos, gadgets and wat-cha-ma-call it's too.

WAYNE B. BOWMAN

Somethings you'd never figure out,

what it was supposed to do.

Thing-a-ma jigs, and silly rigs,

made of metal, glass and wood.

Some things today, I wouldn't say,

even if I could.

So many mysteries in all those buildings,

so many I never found.

Wonderous marvels

that even science professors would astound.

Mr. Shaunnesy was his name.

Fascinating, he could be.

The intelligence of this simple man,

so many could not see.

A computer, a cell phone,

something he never owned.

Couldn't if he wanted to.

For there were no such wonders in 1962.

I traded him a telescope,

for the cranking device I found.

He said it would bring fishing worms,

scampering out of the ground.

So, I followed his advice,

for this interesting device,

and did exactly as I was told.

And within a few cranks,

I was giving thanks,

for more worms than my bucket could hold.

Now, you ask me if this story is true,

knowing that a writer I am.

And here's what I'll say to you.

I'm still thankful to this day,

to have been counted as a friend

of that fascinating old junk man.

TRADITIONAL RHYMING POEMS & SHORT STORIES

TRADITIONAL RHYMING POEMS & SHORT STORIES

CHAPTER 6

SONG LYRICS

TENNESSEE BACKROADS

Walkin' this dusty backroad,
somewhere lost in Tennessee.
Not by accident you know.
Just planned it that way, you see.

Sold my car in Carolina.
All I own is in my pack.

19 west from Ashville.
Never once caught lookin' back.

Don't know where I'm headed.
Doesn't matter anymore.
Guess I'll wake up tomorrow,
somewhere I've never been before.

Played backup for Johnny Cash
Before he passed along.

WAYNE B. BOWMAN

Took advice he once gave me.

And wrote my story in a country song.

Now, everyone has a story.

Some are good and some are bad.

Some will make you smile and laugh.

Still, others will make you sad.

I'll pitch my tent near Knoxville

way back in some evergreens.

Cook dinner on an open fire,

A little bacon and refried beans.

This time tomorrow,

Not sure of where I'll be.

Blessed if ten miles closer

To Nashville Tennessee.

Had a nine to five some time ago.

Not one to be tied down.

So, one day I went out to lunch,

and caught a freight train outta' town.

Walking these lonely backroads

Rain is really pouring down.

Mind so filled with memories

Of yesterday's country sound

They don't write em' like they used to.
Pop country is their thing.
Gone are the days of Hank and Johnny,
steel guitar and western swing.

Well, when I get to heaven,
I know I'll see them all.
Ole' Waylon, George and Merle,
Waitin' for the curtain call.

Someday I'll get to heaven,
But until that day comes.
I'll keep walkin' these dusty backroads
And writin' those country songs.

I'll keep walkin' these dusty backroads
And writin' those country songs.

*(Author note)

Proximo was my first attempt at writing poetry. I was employed part time by a cleaning company that was contracted by a large distillery. These forklift operators were highly skilled in their profession. One night one of them zipped by me with a rap song playing. I found myself getting into the beat and next thing I knew lyrics began to flow. This song is dedicated to all my friends at Proximo Distillery in Lawrenceburg Indiana.

PROXIMO

Now, let me tell you a story of some people I know.

They're the forklift drivers of Proximo.

Well, they're truly skilled in what they do.

You better step aside and let them through.

You know it's easy to rhyme

when words end in "O"

So, I'll give it a run just to put on a show

for the forklift drivers of Proximo.

We are the forklift drivers of Proximo.

We pick up a load and away we go.

It leans to the left; it tilts to the right'

Oops! Now we'll be here all night.

TRADITIONAL RHYMING POEMS & SHORT STORIES

But that's alright
cause we're the forklift drivers of Proximo.

Ya' know we're flyin' around- barely inches to spare.
No fear man, I see you standin' there
just a pushin' that barrel and swishin' that broom.
I'm gonna' zip right past ya' goin zippity zoom.

Do not move cause safety comes first and that's the motto
Of the forklift drivers of Proximo.

Well, there's Lewis, Tyler and Toby too.
Kyle, Mark and Nathan just to mention a few.
Now, they work long hours to earn their pay
Moving tons of product each and every day.

You know they load those trucks one slip at a time
Packed so tight you couldn't wedge a dime.
A job well done, so neat and clean.
What more can I say about this fabulous team?

Now that's all I got man, so what-a-ya think.
Is this pretty good or does it- really stink?

WAYNE B. BOWMAN

A WING AND A PRAYER

You know the day is coming.
Some say that it is near.
Now if you choose to follow,
you have nothing to fear.

For, the good shall be raised,
and the evil they shall fall.
For salvation is free for one and for all.

He's a friend to all those who practice His way,
so, we can go with Him on that glorious day.
I know where I'm going, I hope to see you there.
So, don't put all your hopes on a wing and a prayer.

He gave up His life on the cross for us all.

With outstretched arms, to those who heed the call.
No greater love you see, no man has ever known,
for God's only son now calls us His own.

Now, those are the facts, and how I know them well.
There is a real heaven, there is a real hell.

So, now that you know, then heed what I say.

Take Christ as your Savior and be ready for that day.

So, if you believe and choose to obey,
commit to Him now, be baptized today.
I know where I'm going, and hope to see you there.
So, don't put all your hopes on a wing and a prayer.

So, don't put all your hopes on a wing and a prayer.

WAYNE B. BOWMAN
HIS NAME WAS JESUS

I'd like to tell you a story from a long time ago,
about a man named Jesus, and you should know,
He came to this earth as an innocent child,
bringing peace and salvation to the meek and the mild.

He walked the land teaching peace and love.
Sent by His Father from heaven above.
Spending His time with the sick and the poor,
Until the rich and pious could take it no more.

They were so fearful of His popularity,
His mission here on Earth they failed to see.
Healing the sick and raising the dead.
Nothing but a prophet is what some of them said.

People came from miles away,
to hear what this man of God had to say.
They gathered in towns, on hillsides and by the sea.
Where-ever He roamed, that's where they would be.

For centuries trapped in the bondage of sin.

Now the promised redemption, only through Him.

TRADITIONAL RHYMING POEMS & SHORT STORIES

A message so clear, so don't be deceived.
Hope, and grace for all who believe.

Spread love and forgiveness wherever you go.
His Father in heaven keeps a record, you know.
This message is still as valid today.
His name is Jesus, what more need I say.

WAYNE B. BOWMAN

*(Author's note)

Try this one to a Rap beat.

WHAT HAPPENED TO MY COUNTRY?

Now, I just can't quite understand,

What's going on in this here land,

With all this hatred and all the bigotry.

Now, racism is too often the cry,

And that prompts me to ask the question, why,

When we're all created in our makers image you see.

Well, somewhere back in time some fools,

Decided God had no place in schools,

And things just started to go downhill from there.

So, pretty soon with no moral guide,

Nothin' to keep them on the narrow side

Our kids began to drink, smoke and swear.

Trouble on the way was a guarantee,

When too many shrugged responsibilities,

For teaching our kids that wonderful golden rule.

Treat others as you wish to be,

That works really well for you and me,

And should be taught in every single school.

So, think about this if you will my friend,
Taking God away could bring the end,
Of this great country, this I can foresee.

So, why can't we all just get along,
Turn it around and right the wrong.
To get this done it starts with you and me.

Used to be people cared enough to lend a hand,
And shoulder to shoulder they would stand.
To get the job done, and that was a guarantee.

Cause that's what made this country strong,
And even though sometimes we're wrong,
It's still the home of the brave—and the land of the free.
God bless America!

WAYNE B. BOWMAN

TRADITIONAL RHYMING POEMS & SHORT STORIES

HIS NEVER-ENDING LOVE

Well, my daddy was a miner down in Tennessee.

He always did his best for Momma and me.

He never did complain, worked his fingers to the bone.

Momma would meet him with a kiss at night when he got home.

When you live back in the mountains of east Tennessee,

not a lot of opportunity for the likes of you and me.

not a lot of opportunity for the likes of you and me.

So, you take what you can get, and do without the rest.

And I thank the lord above for His never- ending love.

And I thank the lord above for His never- ending love.

My daddy was a miner way down in Tennessee.

He always did his best for Momma and me.

Now my daddy is gone,

but his memory lingers on.

I remember his love, his never-ending love,

and I thank the Lord above for His never-ending love.

I thank the Lord above for His never-ending love.

WAYNE B. BOWMAN

A COUNTRY CHRISTMAS

It's Christmas in the country.
Gas lanterns light the square.
Decorated cheerful store fronts.
The sound of laughter everywhere.

Children lined up out the doorway,
anxious hearts are waiting there,
for the chance to sit with Santa,
and some secrets with him share.

The snow is gently falling,
on the sidewalks and the streets.
Many smiles and festive wishes,
from everybody that we meet.

Christmas lights light up the square,
softly glistening on the snow.
Vendors booths along the sidewalks,
for the annual Christmas Show.

All the shoppers toting bags,
of toys and gifts, they'll share,

with each other Christmas morning,
and a feast that they've prepared.

I see mom and dad there laughing,
with Mister Morgan in his store.
With two large bags of goodies.
Can't help wonder who there for.

Now, my eyes begin to open.
I realize it's just a dream,
of a Christmas long since passed,
just like yesterday it seemed.

Now, the sound of carolers singing,
bring back memories from the past,
of Christmas in my home town.
Oh, how I hope the memories last.

So, no matter where I travel,
there's no sweeter memory,
then the ones I still remember,
of Christmas in the country.

WAYNE B. BOWMAN
THERE IS A MOUNTAIN

There is a mountain, off in the distance.
It is a mountain, that I must climb.
Someday I'll make it, up to that summit.
My spiritual home there I know I'll find.

I know Gods waiting, up there to welcome,
with open arms into the fold.
He longs to show me, the home He promised,
and countless wonders yet untold.

How far is it, unto that mountain?
As of now I cannot say.
But I assure you, that I am ready,
and looking forward to that day.

When your turn comes, to climb that mountain,
be not afraid, shed not a tear.
For there God waits, with arms wide open,
just as the Bible has made it clear.

TRADITIONAL RHYMING POEMS & SHORT STORIES

ENGINEER BLUES

(Lyrics)

I'm chief engineer on old one twenty-nine.

Well me and my crew, we're always on time.

We run the mountains, valleys, rivers and plains.

Ain't no better life than runnin' these trains.

I got a hand on the throttle, the other slappin' my knee

As we ride the steel through east Tennessee.

I miss my family five days a week.

Four-hour break time to get some sleep.

Four-hour break, time to get some sleep

From coast to coast, and back again.

Someday I'll retire, but I don't know when.

I'll never walk, a mile in another man's shoes,

Though I love what I do, I got the engineer blues.

Ridin' these rails eighty miles an hour.

WAYNE B. BOWMAN

Comin' outta' the curves full throttle power.

Top the ridge and round the bend.

I'll do it all over comin' back again.

I'll do it all over comin' back again.

I'll never walk, a mile in another man's shoes,

Though I love what I do, I got the engineer blues.

I love what I do. I got the engineer blues.

TRADITIONAL RHYMING POEMS & SHORT STORIES

CHAPTER 7

FICTIONAL SHORT STORIES

THE GHOST of MAGGIE VALLEY

I've told this story many times before. But I don't mind repeating it since you asked. It was the most read article I wrote while head reporter at the Greenville North Carolina Observer. I'm ninety-two now, and people still want to hear it.

It was nineteen fifty-six when Noah James Chandler and Emily Louise Stratton first laid eyes on each other. Noah was a senior and Emily a freshman at the high school over there in Waynesville. He was rather tall and handsome with black wavy hair, and she had the most beautiful long black hair that fell well below her shoulders. She had light blue eyes that sparkled when she laughed. Some said it was love at first sight. They were constant companions from then on until Noah enlisted in the Navy for two years. He wanted to learn a trade of some kind so they could get married after his discharge. While in the Navy Noah learned to be a pipe fitter and welder, two very good trades even today. So, they married on June fourth nine-teen sixty and settled into a small rental Airstream travel trailer at Hillbilly Creek-side Campgrounds on the west end of Maggie Valley. Noah worked several small jobs for their first year or so. He was a maintenance man for two different hotels in the area. He then was maintenance man and head janitor over at their old alma mater in Waynesville. They managed to get by with the one income as Emily stayed home taking care of the cooking, cleaning and the various household duties. She loved being a home maker and she was good at it. Home EC' class in high school served her well.

TRADITIONAL RHYMING POEMS & SHORT STORIES

Then one day Noah got a call back from a local contractor he had applied to for a job. They agreed to meet the next day for an interview. Brad Carter took an instant liking to Noah and hired him on the spot. Brads firm had just acquired the contract to build and maintain a new water tower not far from where Noah and Emily now lived. It was to be constructed along Indian Creek. The maintenance contract was a five-year agreement with option to renew. This and other contracts the firm had meant a steady income and stability. Noah could hardly wait to get home and tell Emily. On the way home he stopped at the local clothing store and bought her a pretty blue dress, her favorite color.

Now Carter Maintenance and Construction was a rather small company, so Noah and Emily soon became good friends with the employees and their families. They would have family get togethers from time to time where they would all bring food and the kids would play games and it was a good time for all. Occasionally, Emily and Noah were asked when they thought they might have children. Oh! One of these days maybe. You know, when the good Lord feels the time is right. They had spoken of this from time to time, but felt it would be wise to wait until they had their own place. But, for now they had each other, and they loved one another more than anything in the world.

Noah loved his new job and the people he worked with. Some of his work buddies found great delight in teasing him about various things. For instance, one time they told him the reason he didn't want any kids was because that beautiful wife of his had him spoiled to the point he didn't want to share that attention with anyone else. Harmless fun that would always end with a volley of laughter all around.

Noah and two other men were assigned to do some of the stair welding on the tower. Since he lived nearby, he could

then walk to work weather permitting. Every day Emily would pack him a lunch and set it on the counter by the door. It usually consisted of a lunch meat sandwich, and some fruit for dessert, along with a thermos of coffee. She would always hand him his lunch pail, see him off with a kiss and wishing him a safe day. But on one particular day she was on the phone with her aunt who had been ill for some time. Not wanting to disturb the conversation, he peeked around the corner, waved goodbye and she blew a kiss his way.

He joined the other two men on the third set of stairs to do some weld inspections. This was required prior to painting contractors priming the metal. About mid-morning Noah realized he'd forgot his lunch pail. About ten minutes later he noticed his Ford Expedition coming up from the valley. Emily had seen the lunch box on the counter and was bringing it to Noah. Suddenly, the sound of a horn from his right. A pickup truck coming down the mountain swerves to dodge an elk and side swipes the Expedition causing it to careen through the fence to Indian Creek, some one hundred twenty feet below.

Noah panicked and lost his footing and fell to the steel landing knocking himself unconscious.

"Noah- Noah." Can you hear me, Noah?

"Where am I Brad?"

A man in a doctors outfit says; "That's a good sign. He recognizes you."

"You're in the hospital Noah. You took a spill onto the landing. You sustained a concussion and skull fracture. You're going to be here for a while for observation."

As his mind begins to clear the harsh reality begins to sink in. Scenes begin to flash in his mind. The fear in Emily's face as she slips away. The screams, the horror.

"No! Myy God! Noah screams. Please tell me this is all just a horrible night-mare. I can't live without my Emily."

Brad responds; "I'm so sorry Noah. I'm afraid it's true. Emily is gone."

Four days later, Noah is released from the hospital. Brad is there to take him home. As they enter the small campgrounds, Noah's neighbors assemble to welcome him home. Many offer to help in any way they can.

On the following Monday- Emily Louise (Stratton) Chandler was laid to rest at the Landon Cemetery near where she grew up. A local minister did a beautiful eulogy, ending it with a fitting Twenty-third Psalm. "Yeah, though I walk through the valley of the shadow of death, I will fear no evil."

The gathering was modest. Brad and his entire crew attended. And for the most part the entire campground turned out. Emily's father was killed in a motor cycle accident years ago, and her mother was in a nursing home with a mental disability from the same accident. Noah was comforted and supported by his mother, father and younger sister.

After the service Noah turned down numerous offers for lunch. I just want to be alone now; he would politely explain. And they understood. He needed time to grieve.

Eight months later, he was still grieving. The pain would not go away. He could be seen from time to time setting on a large rock at the edge of Indian Creek just below the tower. He would sometimes appear to be talking to someone, but there was no one there. If you spoke to him in passing, he most often wouldn't answer as if oblivious to his surroundings. As time went by, he grew even more distant. He stopped showing up for work and wouldn't even answer his door or phone.

It was 7:20 AM one morning Brad Carter's phone rang. On the other end was Marvin one of his welders.

"Brad, I'm sorry to have to make this call, but I have some bad news. "

"Why, what is it Marv?"

"It's Noah. When I got here this morning, I found his car in the lot. I called out to him but got no response. Brad, Noah has fallen from the top deck. He's lying at the base of the cliff by the creek. I'm so sorry to have to break this to you."

"Oh, my God! This is just a terrible tragedy."

When Brad arrived at the tower, the rescue team had already retrieved Noah's lifeless body from the creek below. Marv, met Brad at his car and informed him that Noah's safety equipment was still in his car. Local county Sheriff Carl Mason approached the two.

"What a sad day for this community Carl."

"Hi Brad, Marv. It certainly is. What an awful accident."

"Well Carl. I'm not so sure it was an accident."

"You don't think--- What do you mean Brad?"

"Well, for starters, all Noah's safety gear is still in his car. He would have never gone up there without it if he intended to be working on the tower. And there's something else. He has not been the same since losing Emily. She was everything to that man, and I mean everything. And maybe not by coincidence, today is the one-year anniversary of that tragic accident. Maybe Noah just couldn't live with the memory any-more."

"Maybe your right Brad. I'll check his house for any kind of note. But probably won't find anything. Then I'll notify his family."

"Many years have come and gone since then, and the story has been told hundreds of times. And so it goes that throughout the years a number of, mostly credible citizens of Maggie Valley have said that while fishing in the creek or hunting in those mountains they had experienced somewhat of a super natural phenomenon. The locals say if you are fishing or hunting in that area in the early morning hours, when the dew is still on the grass and the fog is hovering low in the valley, you just may see a figure of a young lady in a tattered blue dress kinda' floating through the fog. And if you hear the sound of a woman weeping. Don't be afraid. She won't hurt you. You've just encountered the spirit of Emily Louise Chandler, the ghost of Maggie Valley

Have you seen her?

WAYNE B. BOWMAN

TRADITIONAL RHYMING POEMS & SHORT STORIES

The Waterfall Poet

WAYNE B. BOWMAN

BIOGRAPHY

Bowman, aka; The Waterfall Poet started out writing song lyrics, but soon discovered he enjoyed the rhythmic flow of the rhyming words more so than the melody. "The flow of rhyme can take on a musical feel in and of itself, Bowman says. "Almost something one can dance to without music. After all, what is a song but a collection of words that end in rhyme put to a melody."

I would like to thank first my Almighty Father in Heaven for keeping my family and I in good health during these trying times. Secondly, my wife for allowing me to bounce hundreds of ideas off her, and for her occasional suggestions of subject matter. Writing a book is a lot of work, and her patience is greatly appreciated. And of course, my family and friends for their love and encouragement.

I would also like to thank KDP (Kindle Direct Publishing) and Amazon for their part in the preparation, publishing and marketing of this book. Thank you all.

TRADITIONAL RHYMING POEMS & SHORT STORIES

Special recognition;

Special thanks to Michael J. Masters, MD, of Clyde North Carolina for allowing me access to his Colt revolver for photographic purposes. That photo is shown at the end of the story, "The Man from Tennessee."

Also, I would like to thank Richard and Stacey Boris of Hill Billy Creekside Campground for their sweet southern hospitality during our summer stay in Maggie Valley, North Carolina. We miss you guys.

Other books by this author;

HIDDEN in PLAIN SIGHT – CATECHISM VERSUS the BIBLE

© 2009 Tate Publishing.

Republished ; Kindle Direct Publishing 2023.

*Available from Amazon Books & Kindle Direct Publishing.

Author contact:

waterfallpoet49@gmail.com

TRADITIONAL RHYMING POEMS & SHORT STORIES

TRADITIONAL RHYMING POEMS & SHORT STORIES

Made in the USA
Columbia, SC
12 April 2023